SHOP MANU

MW00784437

Auto Engine Repair

Seventh Edition

Job Sheets for Performance-Based Learning

Chris Johanson
ASE Certified Master Technician

Publisher
The Goodheart-Willcox Company, Inc.
Tinley Park, Illinois
www.g-w.com

Introduction

The *Shop Manual for Auto Engine Repair* provides step-by-step instruction of all the tasks listed in the A1 Engine Repair area of the ASE Education Foundation Task List. Each job in this manual is a hands-on activity, and most jobs correspond to one or more of the ASE Education Foundation tasks. The jobs have been carefully organized and developed to increase your chances of passing the related ASE tests by helping you apply the information you have learned from the *Auto Engine Repair* textbook and in the classroom.

Using this Shop Manual

This shop manual guides you through all the ASE Education Foundation tasks in the A1 Engine Repair area, which include inspecting, testing, and diagnosing starting, charging, lighting, and accessory systems; removing and replacing self-contained components; and removing, overhauling, and reinstalling major components. The jobs are not correlated to specific textbook chapters but will be assigned when your instructor determines that you have sufficient knowledge to complete them.

When performing the jobs, follow these guidelines:
- Read the instructions carefully and proceed through the steps in the order they are presented.
- Refer to the proper service information to find specific procedures and specifications for the vehicle being serviced.
- Carefully read all notes, cautions, and warnings before proceeding.
- Record specifications and the results of diagnostic procedures in the spaces provided.
- Consult your instructor when directed to do so by this shop manual and when unsure of how to proceed.
- Never attempt a step if you are unsure how to perform it correctly.

Features of the Manual

The projects in this manual include a brief introduction about the type of service being performed, a list of the jobs included in the project, a tools and materials list for the jobs, and a list of the ASE Education Foundation tasks that are covered in the project's jobs.

The jobs in this manual are designed to be accomplished in one or two lab sessions. Checkboxes are provided in the left-hand column of the job so you can mark off tasks as they are performed. Blank spaces are provided for recording service-related information.

In addition, three types of special notices appear throughout the jobs in this manual. These notices point out special information or safety considerations for the task being performed. They are color coded according to the type of information being provided:

 Note: Note features provide additional information, special considerations, or professional advice about the task being performed. Note features are blue.

 Caution: Caution features appear near critical steps in a service procedure. These features warn the reader that failure to perform the task properly can lead to equipment or vehicle damage. Caution features are yellow.

 Warning: Warning features also appear near certain critical steps in the service procedure. These features warn the reader that failure to perform the task properly could result in personal injury. Warning features are red.

If properly implemented, this manual will help you do well in your course, pass the related ASE certification tests, and find a job in the automotive industry.

Chris Johanson

Table of Contents

Project 1

Preparing to Service a Vehicle

Introduction

In this project, you will be introduced to some of the tasks that must be completed before a vehicle can be properly serviced. These tasks include evaluating safety considerations, properly identifying the vehicle being serviced, and locating and using appropriate service information.

Thousands of technicians are injured every year while on the job, and some are even killed. Most of these technicians were breaking basic safety rules before their accidents. The technicians that survived learned to respect safety precautions the hard way, by experiencing a painful, but instructive, injury. By studying and following shop safety rules, you can avoid work-related accidents.

The service technician is responsible for maintaining a safe workspace and performing service safely, but is also responsible for protecting the environment. You must follow all applicable environmental laws or risk heavy fines. In addition to the legal obligations, proper waste disposal and recycling will save money. In Job 1, you will locate and identify safety equipment and hazards in the shop. You will also identify the types of wastes generated by the shop and describe the proper procedures for waste disposal.

It is no longer sufficient to open the hood and visually identify an engine. You must use identifying numbers to determine the type of engine and drive train, specifications, part numbers, and which service operations can be performed. Some vehicle systems cannot be successfully serviced without finding and interpreting vehicle numbers. In Job 2, you will locate and interpret vital vehicle numbers.

Once the vehicle and its systems have been properly identified, you must locate the appropriate service information. No technician can do his or her job without knowing how to find, read, and understand service information. Modern service information may come in the form of printed service materials or online resources. In Job 3, you will locate and interpret service information.

With the prevalence of computer-controlled systems, the scan tool is essential for diagnosis. The information retrieved through stored diagnostic trouble codes helps the technician pinpoint problems in computer-controlled systems. In Job 4, you will connect and use a scan tool to retrieve stored trouble codes.

Project 1 Jobs

- Job 1—Perform Safety and Environmental Inspections
- Job 2—Identify and Interpret Vehicle Numbers
- Job 3—Find and Use Service Information
- Job 4—Use a Scan Tool to Retrieve Diagnostic Trouble Codes

Tools and Materials

The following list contains the tools and materials that may be needed to complete the jobs in this project. The items used will depend on the make and model of the vehicle being serviced.

- One or more vehicles.
- Applicable printed service manual.
- A computer and the appropriate service-related software.
- Internet access.
- Technical service bulletin(s).
- Vehicle service history, when available.
- One or more safety data sheets (SDS).
- Other service information.
- Safety glasses and other protective equipment.

Safety Notice

Before performing these jobs, review all pertinent safety information in the text and review safety information with your instructor.

Name _____

Date _____ Class _____

After completing this job, you will be able to locate the shop's fire extinguishers, fire exit, and eye wash stations. You will be able to locate and properly use safety glasses and other shop safety equipment. You will also learn the general safety rules of an auto shop. You will learn the methods of preventing environmental damage through environmentally friendly work procedures.

Instructions

As you read the job instructions, answer the questions and perform the tasks. Record your answers using complete sentences. Ask your instructor for help as needed. A careful study of Chapter 5, *Shop Safety*, will prepare you for some of the procedures in this job.

Warning: Before performing this job, review all pertinent safety information in the text and discuss safety procedures with your instructor.

Procedures

Personal Protective Equipment

☐ 1. Eye protection (safety glasses or goggles) should be worn during any operation that could injure your eyes. See **Figure 1-1**. This includes, for example, hammering, drilling, grinding, and blasting, using compressed air, carrying a battery, or working around a spinning engine fan.

List five common tasks that require the use of safety goggles:

_____

_____

Where are the safety glasses and goggles kept in your shop?

_____

_____

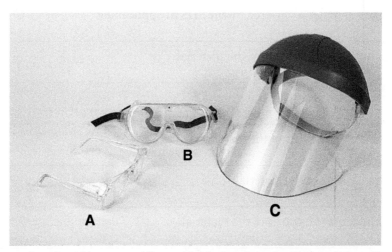

Figure 1-1. Eye protection should be worn while working in the shop. A—Safety glasses. B—Safety goggles. C—Face shield.

☐ 2. Hearing protection (earplugs or protective earmuffs) should be worn during any loud activities. These include tasks like hammering, operating pneumatic tools, and grinding.

List five common tasks that require the use of hearing protection:

_____

_____

Where are the earplugs and protective earmuffs kept in the shop?

_____

_____

☐ 3. Dust masks and respirators may be required performing certain tasks or working with certain chemicals.

Where are respirators and dust masks kept in the shop?

_____

Safety Data Sheets

☐ 1. Walk through the shop and familiarize yourself with the chemicals stored there.

☐ 2. Find the safety data sheets for the chemicals in the shop. Look up information about the chemicals stored in the shop.

Were any chemicals improperly stored according to the safety data sheets?
Yes ____ No ____

If Yes, describe the chemicals and inform your instructor:

_____

Were safety data sheets missing for any of the chemicals in the shop?
Yes ____ No ____

If Yes, describe the chemicals and inform your instructor:

_____

☐ 3. Obtain an SDS from your instructor.

☐ 4. List the following information from the SDS.

General class of material covered by the SDS (if applicable):

_____

Trade (manufacturer's) name for the material:

_____

Chemical or generic name of the material:

_____

Known breathing hazards of the material:

_____

Known fire hazards of the material:

_____

Known skin damage hazards of the material:

_____

Proper storage and disposal methods:

_____

Name _____

Emergency response to spills of the material:

_____

Fire and Shop Safety

☐   1. Walk around the shop and locate all of the fire extinguishers, the fire exit, and fire alarms. Such information is crucial in the event of an emergency.

How many fire extinguishers and alarms are there in your shop?

_____

Where are the fire extinguishers located?

_____

What types of fire extinguishers are available in the shop?

_____

Where are the fire alarms?

_____

How do you leave the shop in case of a fire?

_____

☐   2. To help prevent an emergency, memorize these important fire prevention tips:
- Always take actions to prevent a fire.
- Store gasoline-soaked and oily rags in safety cans, **Figure 1-2**.
- Wipe up spilled gasoline and oil immediately.
- Hold a rag around the fitting when removing a car's fuel line, **Figure 1-3**.

Figure 1-2. Special safety cans should be used to store oily rags.

☐ 3. Identify the location of safety equipment and special hazard areas within the shop. Where are the eye wash stations located?

_____

_____

Where are first aid stations located?

_____

_____

What other special hazard areas exist within the shop?

_____

_____

How are the special hazard areas identified?

_____

_____

Electrical Safety

☐ 1. Check the shop for unsafe electrical conditions, such as damaged electrical cords and overloaded outlets.
Were any unsafe electrical conditions found? Yes ___ No ___
If Yes, describe them in as much detail as possible:

_____

_____

☐ 2. Make sure that all electrically operated tools and equipment with three-prong electrical plugs have their grounding prongs intact, **Figure 1-4**.
Do any tools or equipment have the grounding prong removed? Yes ___ No ___
If Yes, list the items:

_____

⚠ **Warning:** Do not use tools or equipment on which the grounding prong has been removed.

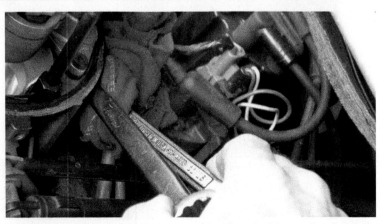

Figure 1-3. This technician is using a shop rag to prevent fuel from leaking as he disconnects a fuel line.

Name _____

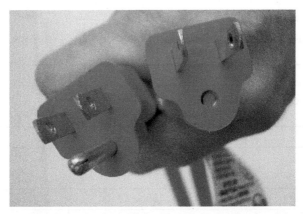

Figure 1-4. The grounding prong has been broken off the electrical plug on the right. Do *not* use a piece of equipment if the grounding prong has been removed.

☐ 3. Obtain the use of a vehicle.

☐ 4. Check the following:

- Battery and battery terminal condition.
- Battery bracket and tray corrosion.
- Ignition secondary wiring condition.
- Condition of all visible wiring.
- Condition of hybrid vehicle high-voltage system wiring.

 Warning: Hybrid high-voltage wires are orange, **Figure 1-5**. Follow all safety precautions when inspecting the insulation and connectors. Remember that these wires carry several hundred volts, and can deliver a lethal shock!

Were any defects found? Yes ___ No ___

If Yes, describe:

_____

_____

Figure 1-5. Be extremely careful when working around the orange high-voltage wires found on hybrid vehicles.

☐ 5. Describe the dangers posed by the following:
Damaged high-voltage wiring insulation:

_____

_____

Loose or corroded connections:

_____

_____

Battery gases:

_____

_____

Short-circuited wiring:

_____

_____

Careless handing of hybrid high-voltage system wiring:

_____

_____

⚠ **Warning:** Other potential sources of high voltage include ignition system secondary wiring, fuel injection system wiring, and high intensity discharge (HID) lighting systems.

Vehicle System-Related Safety Considerations

☐ 1. Identify the special safety considerations associated with each of the following common vehicle systems:
Supplemental restraint systems (SRS):

_____

_____

Electronically controlled braking systems (ABS, TCS):

_____

_____

High intensity discharge (HID) lighting systems:

_____

_____

Compressed Air Safety

☐ 1. Locate the shop's compressed air supply.
What is the air pressure setting on the shop compressor?

_____

Project 1: Job 1 *(continued)*

Describe the dangers posed by compressed air:

_____
_____
_____

Shop Cleanliness

☐ 1. Check the shop floor for unsafe conditions, including spills and trip hazards.
List any unsafe conditions:

_____
_____

☐ 2. Check the shop tools for cleanliness and organization.
List any ways that tool storage can be improved:

_____
_____

Clothing Safety

☐ 1. Different types of gloves are required for different service procedures.
List tasks that require leather gloves:

_____
_____

List tasks that require nitrile gloves:

_____
_____

List tasks that require electrically insulated rubber (electric lineman's) gloves:

_____
_____

List tasks for which mechanic's gloves would be appropriate:

_____
_____

☐ 2. Examine your clothing from a safety standpoint.
List and explain any changes that would make your clothing safer or better-suited in the shop:

_____
_____

☐ 3. Any technicians working in the shop should wear steel-toe safety boots, remove their jewelry, and, if they have long hair, tie it back, out of the way.
In your own words, explain the reasons for these safety precautions:

_____
_____
_____
_____

Carbon Monoxide

☐ 1. Locate the exhaust hoses in the shop.
Where are they located?

_____

_____

☐ 2. Locate the controls to operate the shop's exhaust fans.
Where are they located?

_____

_____

Grinder and Drill Press Safety

☐ 1. Go to the electric grinder and inspect it closely. Locate the power switch. Observe the position of the tool rest and face shield. Also, check the condition of the grinding wheel.
Is the electric grinder in the shop safe? Yes ___ No ___
If No, explain:

_____

_____

☐ 2. Locate and inspect the operation of the shop's drill press. Find the on/off button, feed lever, chuck, and other components.
List the safety precautions associated with operating a drill press:

_____

_____

Floor Jack and Jack Stand Safety

☐ 1. Check out a floor jack and a set of jack stands.

☐ 2. Without lifting a vehicle, practice operating a floor jack. Close the valve on the jack handle. Pump the handle up and down to raise the jack. Then, lower the jack slowly. It is important that you know how to control the lowering action of the jack.
In what direction must you turn the jack handle valve to raise the jack?

_____

To lower the jack?

_____

⚠️ **Warning:** Ask your instructor for permission before beginning the next step. Your instructor may need to demonstrate the procedures to the class.

☐ 3. After getting your instructor's approval, place the jack under a proper lift point on the vehicle (frame, rear axle housing, suspension arm, or reinforced section of the unibody), **Figure 1-6**. If in doubt about where to position the jack, refer to a service manual for the particular vehicle. Instructions will usually be given in one of the front sections of the service information.

Project 1: Job 1 (continued)

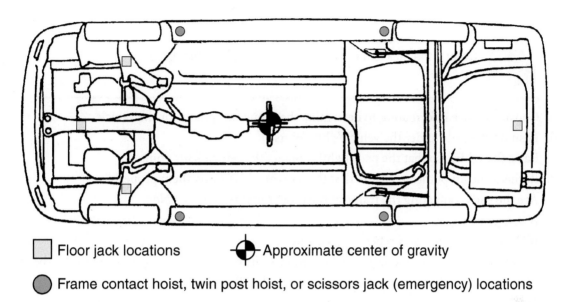

☐ Floor jack locations ⊕ Approximate center of gravity

⬤ Frame contact hoist, twin post hoist, or scissors jack (emergency) locations

Figure 1-6. One manufacturer's recommended lift points are shown here. Consult the proper service literature to determine the lift points for the specific vehicle you are working on.

Where did you position the floor jack?

_____

☐ 4. To raise the vehicle, place the transmission in Neutral and release the emergency brake. This will allow the vehicle to roll as the jack goes up. If the vehicle cannot roll and the small wheels on the jack catch in the shop floor, the vehicle could slide off the jack.

☐ 5. As soon as the vehicle is high enough, place jack stands under the suggested lift points. Lower the vehicle onto the stands slowly. Check that they are safe. Then, remove the floor jack and block the wheels. It should now be safe to work under the car.

Where did you position the jack stands?

_____

☐ 6. Raise the vehicle. Remove the jack stands. Lower the vehicle and return the equipment to the proper storage area.

Hydraulic Lift Safety

☐ 1. Obtain the use of one of the shop's hydraulic lifts.
☐ 2. Without lifting a vehicle, practice operating the lift controls.
☐ 3. Raise the lift and ensure that the lift's safety lock operates properly.

Does the lock operate properly? Yes ___ No ___

If Yes, go to step 4.

If No, consult your instructor before proceeding.

Note: The lift may be equipped with more than one safety lock.

☐ 4. After getting your instructor's approval, drive a vehicle onto the lift.

Note: If the rack is a drive-on type, skip steps 5 through 9.

☐ 5. Consult service information to determine the proper lift points for the vehicle.
☐ 6. Position the pads under the vehicle's lift points.
☐ 7. Raise the vehicle so that the pads lightly contact the vehicle's lift points.
☐ 8. Recheck the lift points to ensure that the pads are contacting them properly.
Are the pads contacting the frame at the proper points? Yes ___ No ___
If Yes, go to step 9.
If No, lower the rack and repeat steps 6 and 7.
☐ 9. Raise the vehicle until the safety lock is engaged. It should now be safe to work under the vehicle.
☐ 10. Make sure all personnel are out from under the lift. Release the safety lock.
☐ 11. Lower the lift.

Environmental Protection

☐ 1. Carefully observe all areas of the shop to see how wastes are produced and stored.
☐ 2. Locate and list the types of solid waste produced.
How are solid wastes disposed of?

_____

_____

☐ 3. Locate and list the types of liquid waste produced.
How are liquid wastes disposed of?

_____

_____

☐ 4. Locate and list types of gases or airborne particles produced.
How are these contaminates prevented from entering the atmosphere?

_____

_____

☐ 5. From the lists above, identify the types of solid and liquid waste that could be recycled:

_____

_____

Identify the materials that could be returned for a core deposit:

_____

_____

Do any Environmental Protection Agency (EPA) regulations apply to the wastes generated in the shop? Yes ___ No ___
If Yes, briefly summarize them:

_____

_____

Name _____

Do any local and state regulations apply to the wastes generated by the shop? Yes ____ No ____
If Yes, briefly summarize them:

_____

_____

List any of the shop's waste disposal practices that require improvement:

_____

_____

Explain what improvements could be made:

_____

_____

☐ 6. Clean the work area and return any equipment to storage.
☐ 7. Did you encounter any problems during this procedure? Yes ____ No ____
If Yes, describe the problems:

_____

_____

What did you do to correct the problems?

_____

_____

☐ 8. Have your instructor check your work and sign this job sheet.

Performance Evaluation—Instructor Use Only

Did the student complete the job in the time allotted? Yes ____ No ____

If No, which steps were not completed? _____

How would you rate this student's overall performance on this job?_____

5–Excellent, 4–Good, 3–Satisfactory, 2–Unsatisfactory, 1–Poor

Comments: _____

_____

_____

INSTRUCTOR'S SIGNATURE_____

Notes

Name _____

Date _____ Class _____

Project 1: Job 2—Identify and Interpret Vehicle Numbers

After completing this job, you will be able to locate and interpret vehicle and vehicle subassembly numbers.

Instructions

As you read the job instructions, answer the questions and perform the tasks. Record your answers using complete sentences. Consult the proper service literature and ask your instructor for help as needed.

Warning: Before performing this job, review all pertinent safety information in the text and discuss safety procedures with your instructor.

Procedures

☐ 1. Obtain a vehicle to be used in this job. Your instructor may specify one or more vehicles to be used.

Locate the Vehicle Identification Number (VIN), Emissions Certification Label, and Refrigerant Identification Label

☐ 1. Locate the vehicle identification number (VIN). On all vehicles built after 1968, the VIN will be visible in the lower driver's side corner of the windshield, **Figure 2-1**. On most vehicles built before 1968, the VIN will be located in the driver's side front door jamb, **Figure 2-2**.

Write the VIN here:

_____

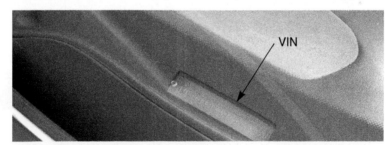

Figure 2-1. On all vehicles made after 1968, the VIN is located on the driver's side of the dashboard, where it can be clearly seen through the windshield.

Figure 2-2. The VIN on this older vehicle is installed inside the driver's side door jamb.

☐ 2. Open the vehicle hood or engine compartment cover and locate the vehicle's emission certification label, **Figure 2-3**.

☐ 3. Answer the following questions:

What is the recommended spark plug gap?

_____

Can the ignition timing be adjusted? Yes ___ No ___

If Yes, what is the recommended base ignition timing?

_____

Is other service information listed on the label? Yes ___ No ___

If Yes, list:

_____

Note: If the vehicle is not equipped with air conditioning, skip the following step. Also, some older air-conditioned vehicles may not have a refrigerant identification label.

☐ 4. Return to the engine compartment and locate the refrigerant identification label, **Figure 2-4**. The refrigerant identification label may be on an air conditioner component or on the inner fender or strut housing.

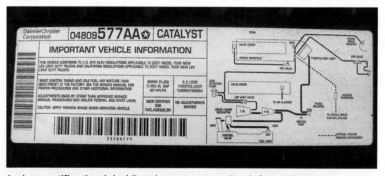

Figure 2-3. The emission certification label lists important service information.

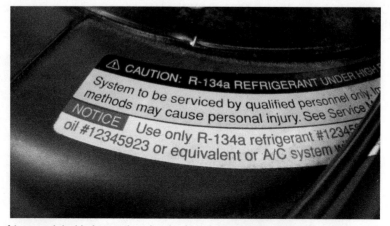

Figure 2-4. The refrigerant label is located under the hood, but not necessarily near any air conditioner components.

Project 2

Removing and Replacing Gaskets and Seals

Introduction

Many service jobs involve replacing gaskets and seals. Gaskets are used throughout the vehicle to hold in engine oil, transmission fluid, gear oil, grease, and coolant. Gaskets are generally durable, but may eventually lose their flexibility and begin to leak. Also, over tightening fasteners can damage a gasket. In Job 5, you will remove and install a gasket.

Lip seals are used throughout the vehicle to seal rotating shafts. A lip seal will be found in each location where a rotating shaft exits a stationary vehicle component. Eventually lip seals wear out and begin leaking. While lip seal replacement is relatively simple, the job must be done properly or the new seal will leak. In Job 6, you will replace a lip seal.

Project 2 Jobs

- Job 5—Remove and Install a Gasket
- Job 6—Remove and Install a Seal

Tools and Materials

The following list contains the tools and materials that may be needed to complete the jobs in this project. The items used will depend on the make and model of the vehicle being serviced.

- One or more vehicles.
- Applicable service information.
- Drain pan.
- Gasket scraper.
- Replacement gasket.
- Gasket sealer or adhesive.
- Housing in need of pressed-in lip seal replacement.
- Lip seal removal tool.
- Seal driver.
- Replacement seal.
- Nonhardening sealer.
- Hand tools.
- Air-powered tools.
- Safety glasses and other protective equipment.

Safety Notice

Before performing these jobs, review all pertinent safety information in the text and review safety information with your instructor.

Project 2: Job 5—Remove and Install a Gasket

After completing this job, you will be able to remove and install a gasket on an automotive part.

Instructions

As you read the job instructions, answer the questions and perform the tasks. Record your answers using complete sentences. Consult the proper service literature and ask your instructor for help as needed.

> ⚠ **Warning:** Before performing this job, review all pertinent safety information in the text and discuss safety procedures with your instructor.

Procedures

☐ 1. Obtain a vehicle to be used in this job. Your instructor may direct you to perform this job on a shop vehicle or engine.

☐ 2. Gather the tools needed to perform the following job. Refer to the tools and materials list at the beginning of the project.

Remove a Gasket

☐ 1. Make sure all lubricant has been drained from the unit containing the part and gasket to be removed.

> **Note:** Skip the preceding step if the lubricant does not cover the part to be removed when the vehicle is not running. Care should be taken that the lubricant is not contaminated with gasket material or other foreign material during this task.

☐ 2. Remove the part covering the gasket. You may need to lightly pry the parts apart. Be very careful not to damage the sealing surfaces.

☐ 3. Scrape all old gasket material from both sealing surfaces.

☐ 4. Thoroughly clean the removed part and remove any gasket material or other debris on the related components in the vehicle.

☐ 5. Inspect for gouges, cracks, dents, and warped areas on the sealing surfaces of the removed part and assembly to which it attaches.

Describe the condition of the sealing surfaces of the removed part and the corresponding surfaces on the vehicle:

_____

_____

☐ 6. Repair or replace the parts if defects are found.

Install a Gasket

☐ 1. Obtain a replacement gasket and compare it with the part's sealing surface. See **Figure 5-1**. Make sure that the following conditions are met:

- The replacement gasket is the correct size and shape. ___

- The gasket material is correct for this application. ___

☐ 2. Place a light coat of sealer or adhesive, as applicable, on the removed part to hold the gasket in place during reinstallation.

 Note: Sealer may not be needed on all applications. Check the service manual for specific instructions.

☐ 3. Place the gasket in place on the part.
☐ 4. Reinstall the part, being careful not to damage or misalign the gasket.
☐ 5. Install the fasteners. Do not tighten any fastener until all fasteners are started.
☐ 6. Tighten all fasteners to the correct torque. Follow these rules to avoid gasket damage and leaks:

- Tighten the fasteners in the manufacturer's sequence. If a sequence is not available, follow the procedures shown in **Figure 5-2**. If the part is irregularly shaped, start from the innermost fasteners and work outward.

- Tighten each fastener slightly, then move to the next fastener. Repeat the sequence until final torque is reached.

- Be especially careful not to overtighten fasteners holding sheet metal components.

- Rubber gaskets, sometimes called "spaghetti gaskets," require very low torque values. **Figure 5-3** shows a typical spaghetti gasket. Be extremely careful not to overtighten these types of gaskets.

☐ 7. Add the correct type and amount of fresh lubricant into the unit as needed.

Figure 5-1. Compare the new gasket to the part-sealing surface to ensure that it is correct.

Name_____

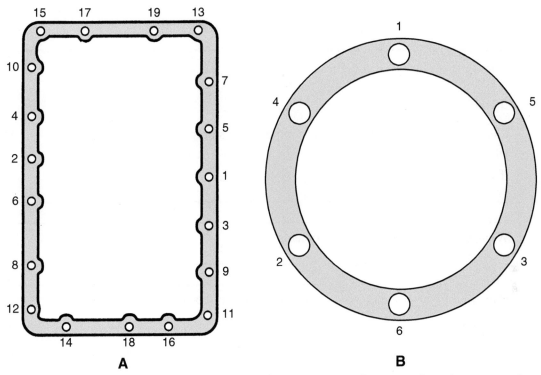

Figure 5-2. A—When tightening a square or rectangular pan or cover, always start from the center and work outward. This allows the gasket to spread out, improving the seal. B—When installing the fasteners on a round cover, tighten in a star or crisscross pattern.

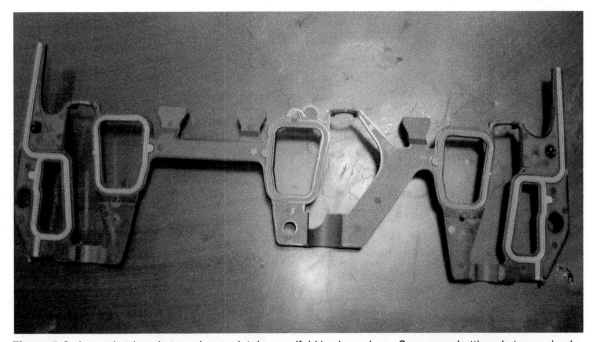

Figure 5-3. A spaghetti gasket used on an intake manifold is shown here. Some spaghetti gaskets are simply sections of flexible rubber that strongly resemble spaghetti. They are extremely easy to overtighten.

> **Note:** If there is any possibility that the lubricant was contaminated during the gasket replacement process, it should be replaced.

☐ 8. Operate the vehicle and check for leaks.

Job Wrap-Up

☐ 1. Clean the work area and return any equipment to storage.

☐ 2. Did you encounter any problems during this procedure? Yes ___ No ___
If Yes, describe the problems:

_____

_____

What did you do to correct the problems?

_____

_____

☐ 3. Have your instructor check your work and sign this job sheet.

Performance Evaluation—Instructor Use Only

Did the student complete the job in the time allotted? Yes ___ No ___

If No, which steps were not completed? _____

How would you rate this student's overall performance on this job?_____

5–Excellent, 4–Good, 3–Satisfactory, 2–Unsatisfactory, 1–**Poor**

Comments: _____

_____

_____

INSTRUCTOR'S SIGNATURE_____

Name_____

Date _____ Class _____

After completing this job, you will be able to replace a pressed-in lip seal.

Instructions

As you read the job instructions, answer the questions and perform the tasks. Record your answers using complete sentences. Consult the proper service literature and ask your instructor for help as needed.

> ⚠ **Warning:** Before performing this job, review all pertinent safety information in the text and discuss safety procedures with your instructor.

Procedures

☐ 1. Obtain a vehicle to be used in this job. Your instructor may direct you to perform this job on a shop vehicle or engine.

☐ 2. Gather the tools needed to perform the following job. Refer to the tools and materials list at the beginning of the project.

Remove a Seal

☐ 1. Remove shafts and other parts that restrict access to the lip seal to be replaced.

> 🔧 **Caution:** Drain oil to a level below the seal if necessary.

☐ 2. Remove the lip seal by one of the following methods:
- Prying the seal from the housing. See **Figure 6-1**.
- Driving the seal from the back side of the housing.

Figure 6-1. If the seal will not be reused, pry it from the housing with a large screwdriver or pry bar. Be careful not to damage the seal housing during removal.

- Using a special removal tool to remove the seal.

Describe the method used to remove the lip seal.

_____

☐ 3. Obtain a replacement seal and compare it with the old seal.

Is the replacement seal correct? Yes ___ No ___

If No, what should you do next?

_____

_____

Install a Seal

☐ 1. Thoroughly clean the seal housing to remove oil, sludge and carbon deposits, and old sealer.

☐ 2. Inspect the seal housing for cracks, gouges, and dents at the sealing area. **Figure 6-2** shows a cracked seal housing.

Describe the condition of the housing and the old seal:

_____

_____

☐ 3. Inspect the shaft at the sealing area. Look for nicks, burrs, and groove wear.

Describe the condition of the shaft at the sealing area:

_____

_____

Figure 6-2. This seal housing is visibly cracked. A damaged seal housing must be properly repaired or replaced.

Name _____

 Note: Defective housings should be repaired or replaced. Defective shafts should also be replaced. Consult your instructor to determine what additional steps, if any, need to be taken.

☐ 4. Lightly lubricate the lip of the seal as shown in **Figure 6-3**. Use the same type of lubricant as is used in the device being serviced.

☐ 5. If specified by the seal manufacturer, lightly coat the outside diameter of the seal with nonhardening sealer.

☐ 6. Install the new seal using one of the following methods:

  • Drive the seal into place with a seal driver, **Figure 6-4**.

  • Carefully tap the seal into place with a hammer.

Figure 6-3. Lubricate the sealing lip before installation.

Figure 6-4. A typical seal driver.

Caution: When installing a seal by tapping it into place with a hammer, lightly tap on alternating sides of the seal.

Describe the method used to install the seal:

_____

_____

Caution: Some technicians prefer to drive the seal into place using a hammer and a block of wood. This should only be done when no other method is available. Wood fragments can enter the bore and cause damage.

☐   7. Reinstall the shaft and other parts as necessary.

☐   8. Check that the shaft turns freely after all parts are installed.

☐   9. Add fluid as needed. Then, operate the unit and check for leaks.

Job Wrap-Up

☐   1. Clean the work area and return any equipment to storage.

☐   2. Did you encounter any problems during this procedure? Yes ___ No ___
If Yes, describe the problems:

_____

_____

What did you do to correct the problems?

_____

_____

☐   3. Have your instructor check your work and sign this job sheet.

Performance Evaluation—Instructor Use Only

Did the student complete the job in the time allotted? Yes ___ No ___

If No, which steps were not completed? _____

How would you rate this student's overall performance on this job?_____

5–Excellent, 4–Good, 3–Satisfactory, 2–Unsatisfactory, 1–Poor

Comments: _____

_____

_____

INSTRUCTOR'S SIGNATURE_____

Project 3

Inspecting, Replacing, and Aligning Power Train Mounts

Introduction

A broken or misaligned power train mount can cause several problems. Misaligned power train mounts can cause noises, vibration, or pulling on acceleration. A broken or misaligned power train mount can cause an engine or drive train part to strike the body. You will inspect power train mounts in Job 7, and then replace and align them in Job 8.

Project 3 Jobs

- Job 7—Inspect Power Train Mounts
- Job 8—Replace and Align Power Train Mounts

Tools and Materials

The following list contains the tools and materials that may be needed to complete the jobs in this project. The items used will depend on the make and model of the vehicle being serviced.

- Vehicle needing power train mount service.
- Applicable service information.
- Pry bars.
- Engine lifting fixture (not always needed).
- Droplight or other source of illumination.
- Hand tools.
- Safety glasses and other protective equipment.

Safety Notice

Before performing these jobs, review all pertinent safety information in the text and review safety information with your instructor.

Notes

Project 3: Job 7—Inspect Power Train Mounts

After completing this job, you will be able to check power train mounts on front- and rear-wheel drive vehicles.

Instructions

As you read the job instructions, answer the questions and perform the tasks. Record your answers using complete sentences. Consult the proper service literature and ask your instructor for help as needed.

> **Warning:** Before performing this job, review all pertinent safety information in the text and discuss safety procedures with your instructor.

Procedures

☐ 1. Obtain a vehicle to be used in this job. Your instructor may direct you to perform this job on a shop vehicle.

☐ 2. Gather the tools needed to perform the following job. Refer to the tools and materials list at the beginning of the project.

Preliminary Check

☐ 1. Open the hood of the vehicle.

> **Caution:** Before performing any work under the hood of a vehicle, always place covers over the fenders to prevent scratches and dings.

☐ 2. Apply the parking brake.

☐ 3. Have an assistant start the engine and tightly press on the brake pedal while placing the engine in drive.

> **Note:** If the engine rises more than 1″ (25 mm) in the following steps, a motor mount may be broken or soft. If this occurs, make a visual inspection of the mounts using the procedure presented later in this job.

☐ 4. Have the assistant slightly open the throttle.

☐ 5. Observe the engine.

Does the engine move excessively (more than 1″, or 25 mm)? Yes ____ No ____

If Yes, perform a visual inspection of the motor mounts.

> **Note:** While checking the mounts, look for shiny places where the paint has been worn away on the frame, body, and underside of the hood. These places indicate that the engine is moving excessively and contacting these parts.

☐ 6. Continue to observe the engine as you have your assistant place the transmission in reverse and slightly open the throttle while keeping the brakes engaged.

Did the engine move excessively? Yes ___ No ___

If Yes, perform a visual inspection of the motor mounts.

Visual Inspection

☐ 1. Make sure that there is sufficient illumination to see the mount. If necessary, have an assistant hold a light in position to illuminate the mount. Mount locations vary. **Figure 7-1** and **Figure 7-2** show the general location of motor and drive train mounts on front-wheel and rear-wheel drive vehicles.

☐ 2. With the engine off, carefully pry on the engine to raise it in the area of a solid mount. Check for cracked rubber in the mount as the engine moves. Note the damage shown in **Figure 7-3**.

Do you find any cracked rubber in the mount? Yes ___ No ___

If Yes, replace the mount using the procedures outlined in Job 8.

☐ 3. Check fluid-filled mounts for exterior oil leakage.

Do you detect any oil leakage? Yes ___ No ___

If Yes, replace the mount using the procedures outlined in Job 8.

☐ 4. Check the mounts for loose fasteners.

Do you find any loose fasteners? Yes ___ No ___

If Yes, tighten the fasteners to the proper torque.

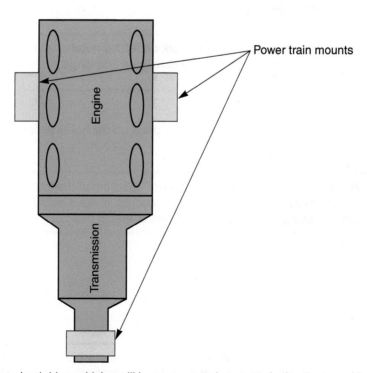

Figure 7-1. Most rear-wheel drive vehicles will have power train mounts in these general locations.

Name _____

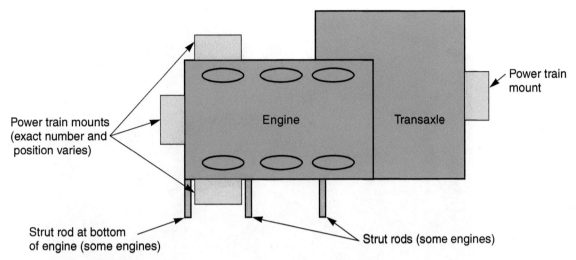

Figure 7-2. Typical locations for power train mounts on a front-wheel drive vehicle. Mount locations on front-wheel drive vehicles vary between makers, and even between engines from the same maker. Always check the service literature for the exact mount locations.

Note: Before returning a vehicle to a customer, always inspect the work area and passenger compartment to ensure that all tools, parts, and debris related to the service have been picked up. Some companies may want the disposable floor mats and protective covers left in place until the customer takes possession of the vehicle. Always prepare the vehicle in accordance with your company or school's policy.

Job Wrap-Up

☐ 1. Clean the work area and return any equipment to storage.

☐ 2. Did you encounter any problems during this procedure? Yes ___ No ___
   If Yes, describe the problems:

   _____

   _____

   What did you do to correct the problems?

   _____

   _____

☐ 3. Have your instructor check your work and sign this job sheet.

Figure 7-3. Typical power train mount damage.

Performance Evaluation—Instructor Use Only

Did the student complete the job in the time allotted? Yes ___ No ___

If No, which steps were not completed? _____

How would you rate this student's overall performance on this job?_____

5–Excellent, 4–Good, 3–Satisfactory, 2–Unsatisfactory, 1–Poor

Comments: _____

_____

_____

INSTRUCTOR'S SIGNATURE_____

Project 3: Job 8—Replace and Align Power Train Mounts

After completing this job, you will be able to replace and align power train mounts on front- and rear-wheel drive vehicles.

Instructions

As you read the job instructions, answer the questions and perform the tasks. Record your answers using complete sentences. Consult the proper service literature and ask your instructor for help as needed.

> ⚠ **Warning:** Before performing this job, review all pertinent safety information in the text and discuss safety procedures with your instructor.

Procedures

- ☐ 1. Obtain a vehicle to be used in this job. Your instructor may direct you to perform this job on a shop vehicle.
- ☐ 2. Gather the tools needed to perform the following job. Refer to the tools and materials list at the beginning of the project.

Replace Power Train Mounts

> ⚠ **Warning:** The vehicle must be raised and supported in a safe manner. Always use an approved lift or jack and jack stands.

- ☐ 1. Raise the vehicle as necessary to gain access to the power train mount to be replaced.
- ☐ 2. Place a jack stand under the engine or transmission/transaxle near the power train mount to be replaced. On some front-wheel drive vehicles, an engine-lifting device can be used to raise the engine and remove pressure on the mounts.

> 🔧 **Caution:** Place the jack stand so that it will not damage the underside of the engine or transmission/transaxle. If necessary, place a wood block or other protective device on the jack stand.

- ☐ 3. Lower the vehicle just enough to remove the weight of the engine and drive train from the mount to be replaced.
- ☐ 4. Lightly shake the vehicle to ensure that the jack stand is solidly placed.
- ☐ 5. Remove the fasteners holding the mount to the engine and vehicle.
- ☐ 6. Compare the old and new mounts to ensure that the new mount is correct.
- ☐ 7. Place the new mount in position and install the fasteners loosely.
- ☐ 8. Once all fasteners are in place, tighten them to the proper torque.

  What is the proper fastener torque? _____

- ☐ 9. Raise the vehicle and remove the jack stand.

☐ 10. If necessary, align the new power train mount using the procedure in the next section(s).

Adjust Power Train Mounts on Rear-Wheel Drive Vehicles

Note: Many rear-wheel drive power train mounts are not adjustable. Some rear mounts can be shimmed to correct drive shaft angle problems.

☐ 1. Loosen the mounting bolts.
☐ 2. Move the tailshaft until it is centered in the drive shaft tunnel.
☐ 3. Retighten the mounting bolts.
   What is the proper fastener torque? _____

Adjust Power Train Mounts on Front-Wheel Drive Vehicles

☐ 1. Observe the marks made by the cradle mounting bolts and washers. If the original marks made by the washers are not completely covered, the cradle is incorrectly positioned.
   Is the cradle properly positioned? Yes ___ No ___

Note: If the cradle is correctly positioned, skip to step 5.

☐ 2. Loosen the cradle fasteners.
☐ 3. Move the cradle to its original position.
☐ 4. Tighten the cradle fasteners.
☐ 5. Measure the mount adjustment. On many vehicles, mount adjustment is checked by measuring the length of the CV axle on the same side as the adjustable mount. If the length of the CV axle is correct, the mount is properly adjusted. On other vehicles the difference between the mount and a stationary part of the vehicle frame must be measured. Sometimes the only procedure is to loosen the fasteners and allow the mount to assume its normal unloaded position.
   Briefly describe the mount adjustment method:

   _____

   _____

   _____

   Is the mount adjustment correct? Yes ___ No ___
   If Yes, and with your instructor's approval, skip to step 12.
☐ 6. Remove the load on the mount by raising the engine and transaxle assembly with a floor jack.

Caution: Raise the assembly only enough to unload the mount. Be careful not to damage the oil pan.

☐ 7. Loosen the adjustable mount fasteners.

Project 3: Job 8 *(continued)*

☐   8.   Reposition the mount as needed.

☐   9.   Lower the floor jack.

☐   10.   Measure the mount using the same method used in step 5.

     Is the mount adjustment correct? Yes ___ No ___

     If No, repeat steps 6 through 10.

☐   11.   Tighten the mount fasteners.

     What is the proper fastener torque?

_____

☐   12.   Remove the jack from under the engine and transaxle.

Job Wrap-Up

☐   1.   Clean the work area and return any equipment to storage.

☐   2.   Did you encounter any problems during this procedure? Yes ___ No ___

     If Yes, describe the problems:

_____

_____

     What did you do to correct the problems?

_____

_____

☐   3.   Have your instructor check your work and sign this job sheet.

Performance Evaluation—Instructor Use Only

Did the student complete the job in the time allotted? Yes ___ No ___

If No, which steps were not completed? _____

How would you rate this student's overall performance on this job?_____

5–Excellent, 4–Good, 3–Satisfactory, 2–Unsatisfactory, 1–Poor

Comments: _____

_____

_____

INSTRUCTOR'S SIGNATURE_____

Notes

Project 4

Lubrication System Inspection and Service

Introduction

Periodic oil and filter changes can greatly prolong the life of an engine. Oil and filter changes are relatively simple, but must be done correctly. It is also vital that any oil or coolant leaks be found and promptly fixed. Oil pressure and temperature sensors indicate when there is a problem with the lubrication system. It is extremely important that these components function properly. In Job 9, you will drain and replace the engine oil and change the oil filter. In Job 10, you will observe the engine for oil, coolant, and fuel leaks. In Job 11, you will inspect, test, and replace oil temperature and oil pressure sensors and switches.

Project 4 Jobs

- Job 9—Change Oil and Filter
- Job 10—Inspect an Engine for Leaks
- Job 11—Inspect, Test, and Replace Oil Temperature and Oil Pressure Sensors and Switches

Tools and Materials

The following list contains the tools and materials that may be needed to complete the jobs in this project. The items used will depend on the make and model of the vehicle being serviced.

- Vehicle in need of service.
- Applicable service information.
- Oil filter wrench.
- Oil drain pan.
- Oil filter.
- Correct type and grade of oil.
- Leak detection equipment.
- Shop towels.
- Hand tools.
- Safety glasses and other protective equipment.

Safety Notice

Before performing these jobs, review all pertinent safety information in the text and review safety information with your instructor.

Project 4:   Job 9—Change Oil and Filter

After completing this job, you will be able to perform an oil and filter change.

Instructions

As you read the job instructions, answer the questions and perform the tasks. Record your answers using complete sentences. Consult the proper service literature and ask your instructor for help as needed.

> ⚠ **Warning:** Before performing this job, review all pertinent safety information in the text and discuss safety procedures with your instructor.

Procedures

☐ 1. Obtain a vehicle to be used in this job. Your instructor may direct you to perform this job on a shop vehicle or engine.

☐ 2. Gather the tools needed to perform the following job. Refer to the tools and materials list at the beginning of the project.

☐ 3. Obtain the correct oil filter and type and grade of motor oil.

Brand, grade, and weight of oil:

_____

Brand and stock number of oil filter:

_____

☐ 4. Run the engine until it reaches operating temperature.

☐ 5. Raise the vehicle on a lift or raise it with a jack and secure it on jack stands. The vehicle should be level when raised to allow all of the oil to drain from the pan.

> ⚠ **Warning:** The vehicle must be raised and supported in a safe manner. Always use approved lifts or jacks and jack stands.

☐ 6. Place the oil drain pan under the engine oil pan. **Figure 9-1** shows a typical oil drain pan.

☐ 7. Remove the oil drain plug. A few engines have two drain plugs.

> ⚠ **Warning:** Avoid contact with hot oil. You could be severely burned.

☐ 8. Inspect the drain plug. The seal should be undamaged to prevent leaks. Check the drain plug's threads for damage. If the drain plug is damaged, replace it.

Are the drain plug threads and seal OK? Yes ____ No ____

☐ 9. Loosen the oil filter using a filter wrench and remove the filter from the engine. If necessary, reposition the oil drain pan under the filter or use a second drain pan.

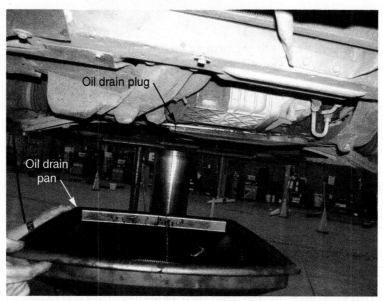

Figure 9-1. The oil pan should be large enough to fit under both the oil drain and the oil filter.

- [ ] 10. Wipe off the oil filter mounting base and check that the old filter seal is not stuck on the base.
- [ ] 11. Check the new filter to ensure that it is the correct replacement.
- [ ] 12. Fill the new filter with the correct grade of motor oil. If the oil filter is mounted with the opening down, skip this step.
- [ ] 13. Smear a thin film of clean engine oil on to the new oil filter rubber seal as shown in **Figure 9-2**.
- [ ] 14. Screw on the new oil filter and hand tighten it.
- [ ] 15. Turn the filter an additional 1/2 to 3/4 turn.
- [ ] 16. Install and tighten the oil drain plug.
- [ ] 17. Remove the oil filler cap from the engine.

Figure 9-2. Use clean oil to lightly lubricate the filter seal.

Name _____

☐ 18. Open the first oil container and pour the oil into the filler opening in the engine. Carefully monitor the filler opening to ensure that oil does not spill out.

☐ 19. Repeat step 18 until the engine is filled to the proper level.

☐ 20. Replace the filler cap and wipe any spilled oil from the engine.

☐ 21. Start the engine and watch the oil pressure light or gauge. The light should go out or the gauge should begin to register within 10 to 20 seconds. If it does not, stop the engine immediately and locate the problem.

☐ 22. Raise the vehicle and check for leaks from the oil filter and drain plug.

Are there any leaks? Yes ___ No ___

If you found leaks, what did you do to correct them?

_____

_____

_____

☐ 23. Lower the vehicle and stop the engine.

☐ 24. Allow the engine to sit for several minutes.

☐ 25. Recheck the oil level.

Is the level correct? Yes ___ No ___

If the level is low, add oil until the dipstick reads full.

Job Wrap-Up

☐ 1. Clean the work area and return any equipment to storage. Dispose of the old oil filter properly, **Figure 9-3**.

Figure 9-3. Always dispose of the old oil filter in special oil filter containers. The oil filters are disposed of without damaging the environment.

☐ 2. Did you encounter any problems during this procedure? Yes ___ No ___
     If Yes, describe the problems:

     _____

     _____

     What did you do to correct the problems?

     _____

     _____

☐ 3. Have your instructor check your work and sign this job sheet.

Performance Evaluation—Instructor Use Only

Did the student complete the job in the time allotted? Yes ___ No ___

If No, which steps were not completed? _____

How would you rate this student's overall performance on this job?_____

5–Excellent, 4–Good, 3–Satisfactory, 2–Unsatisfactory, 1–Poor

Comments: _____

_____

_____

INSTRUCTOR'S SIGNATURE_____

Project 4: Job 10—Inspect an Engine for Leaks

After completing this job, you will be able to check an engine for leaks.

Instructions

As you read the job instructions, answer the questions and perform the tasks. Record your answers using complete sentences. Consult the proper service literature and ask your instructor for help as needed.

> ⚠️ **Warning:** Before performing this job, review all pertinent safety information in the text and discuss safety procedures with your instructor.

Procedures

☐ 1. Obtain a vehicle to be used in this job. Your instructor may direct you to perform this job on a shop vehicle or engine.

☐ 2. Gather the tools needed to perform the following job. Refer to the tools and materials list at the beginning of the project.

Visual Inspection

☐ 1. Inspect the top of the engine for leaks. Such leaks will usually be visible at the point of leakage.
- Common upper-engine oil leak points are valve covers, timing covers, and the oil filler cap.

Are any oil leaks found? Yes ___ No ___

If Yes, list the locations of the oil leaks:

_____

- Common upper-engine fuel leak points are fuel fittings, hose clamps, and pressure regulators.

Are any fuel leaks found? Yes ___ No ___

If Yes, list the locations of the fuel leaks:

_____

- Common upper-engine coolant leak points are hoses, hose fittings, radiator seams, and the radiator cap. **Figure 10-1** shows a leak visible at the thermostat housing and hose connection.

Are any coolant leaks found? Yes ___ No ___

If Yes, list the locations of the coolant leaks:

_____

> **Note:** Pressure testing the cooling system is covered in Job 35.

☐ 2. Obtain a drop light or other source of illumination.

☐ 3. Examine the underside of the vehicle for evidence of oil or grease. Slight seepage is normal. **Figure 10-2** shows a valve cover leak that is causing oil to flow down the rear of the head and block.

Is excessive oil or grease observed? Yes ___ No ___

If Yes, where does the oil/grease appear to be coming from?

_____

 Note: Airflow under the vehicle will blow leaking oil backward. The leak may be some distance forward from where the oil appears.

Powder Method

☐ 1. Thoroughly clean the area around the suspected leak.

☐ 2. Apply talcum powder to the clean area.

☐ 3. Lower the vehicle from the lift and drive it several miles or carefully run it on the lift for 10–15 minutes.

☐ 4. Raise the vehicle (if necessary) and check the area around the suspected leak.

Figure 10-1. Coolant leaks often occur at the thermostat housing and hose. They can usually be spotted by the presence of coolant on the manifold or directly under the housing.

Figure 10-2. This oil leak could have been misdiagnosed. Oil leaking from the top of the engine is often blamed on seals on the bottom of the engine.

Project 4: Job 10 (continued)

 Warning: The vehicle must be raised and supported in a safe manner. Always use approved lifts or jacks and jack stands.

Does the powder show streaks of oil, fuel, or coolant? Yes ___ No ___

If Yes, which type of fluid is leaking and where does it appear to be coming from?

_____

Black Light Method

☐ 1. Ensure that the engine has enough oil and coolant. Add oil or coolant as needed.

☐ 2. Add fluorescent dye to the unit through the filler plug, being careful not to spill dye on the outside of the engine.

☐ 3. Lower the vehicle from the lift and drive it several miles, or carefully run it on the lift for 10–15 minutes.

☐ 4. Raise the vehicle, if necessary.

 Warning: The vehicle must be raised and supported in a safe manner. Always use approved lifts or jacks and jack stands.

☐ 5. Turn on the black light and direct it toward the area around the suspected leak. See **Figure 10-3**.

Does the black light show the presence of dye? Yes ___ No ___

If Yes, where does the dye appear to be coming from?

_____

☐ 6. Consult your instructor about the steps to take to correct the leak. Steps may include the following:

- Tightening fasteners.
- Replacing gaskets or seals. See Jobs 5 and 6.
- Replacing a cracked, broken, or punctured part.

Figure 10-3. When necessary, a black light can be used to locate leaks. (Tracer Products Division of Spectronics Corporation)

Steps to be taken:

_____

_____

☐ 7. Make the necessary repairs.

Job Wrap-Up

☐ 1. Clean the work area and return any equipment to storage.

☐ 2. Did you encounter any problems during this procedure? Yes ___ No ___
If Yes, describe the problems:

_____

_____

What did you do to correct the problems?

_____

_____

☐ 3. Have your instructor check your work and sign this job sheet.

Performance Evaluation—Instructor Use Only

Did the student complete the job in the time allotted? Yes ___ No ___

If No, which steps were not completed? _____

How would you rate this student's overall performance on this job?_____

5–Excellent, 4–Good, 3–Satisfactory, 2–Unsatisfactory, 1–Poor

Comments: _____

_____

_____

INSTRUCTOR'S SIGNATURE_____

Project 4:   Job 11—Inspect, Test, and Replace Oil Temperature and Oil Pressure Sensors and Switches

After completing this job, you will be able to inspect, test, and replace oil temperature and oil pressure sensors and switches.

Instructions

As you read the job instructions, answer the questions and perform the tasks. Record your answers using complete sentences. Consult the proper service literature and ask your instructor for help as needed.

> ⚠️ **Warning:** Before performing this job, review all pertinent safety information in the text and discuss safety procedures with your instructor.

Procedures

☐ 1. Obtain a vehicle to be used in this job. Your instructor may direct you to perform this job on a shop vehicle.

☐ 2. Gather the tools needed to perform this job. Refer to the tools and materials list at the beginning of the project.

> ⚠️ **Warning:** Electronic circuits on late-model vehicles can be destroyed by careless use of jumper cables or electrical test equipment. Always consult the manufacturer's service information and wiring diagrams before performing any of the following tests.

Switch- and Sensor-Operated Warning Lights

There are two kinds of warning light problems:
- The warning light is on at all times.
- The warning light does not light at any time.

Refer to the appropriate section of this job based on the type of problem you are diagnosing.

Warning Light Is Always On

> **Note:** This procedure assumes that the vehicle has no engine problems that would illuminate the light.

☐ 1. Turn the ignition switch to the *On* position.

☐ 2. Locate the switch or sensor on the engine, **Figure 11-1**.

☐ 3. Unplug the connector at the switch or sensor.

Does the light go out? Yes ____ No ____

If Yes, the sender is defective.

If No, there is another electrical problem in the vehicle. Look for a wire that has grounded against the vehicle body or other problem.

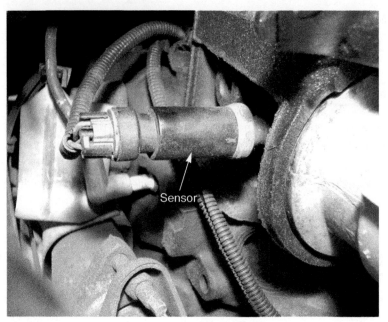

Figure 11-1. Many oil pressure sensors are located near the oil filter.

Warning Light Does Not Light

☐ 1. Check the fuse.

Is the fuse blown or missing? Yes ___ No ___

If Yes, determine the cause, correct it, and recheck warning light operation.

If No, continue on to step 2.

☐ 2. Unplug the connector at the switch or sensor.

☐ 3. Using a fused jumper wire, ground the switch or sensor connector.

Does the light come on? Yes ___ No ___

If Yes, the sender is defective.

If No, there is another electrical problem in the vehicle. Look for an open or disconnected wire, or a burned out or disconnected bulb.

 Note: In some cases, someone has removed the bulb because the light was always on. If this is the case, install a new bulb and then find out why the light is on all of the time using the procedure in the *Warning Light Is Always On* section of this job.

Switch- and Sensor-Operated Gauges

☐ 1. Check the fuse.

Is the fuse blown or missing? Yes ___ No ___

If Yes, determine the cause, correct it, and recheck gauge operation.

If No, continue to step 2.

☐ 2. Turn the ignition to the *On* position.

Project 4: Job 11 *(continued)*

☐ 3. Note the gauge reading. **Figure 11-2** shows an oil pressure gauge that is believed to be defective.

☐ 4. Remove the switch or sensor connector.

Does this cause a change in the gauge reading? Yes ___ No ___

If Yes, go to step 6.

If No, go to step 5.

☐ 5. Ground the gauge switch or sensor connector to the body, **Figure 11-3**.

Does this cause a change in the gauge reading? See **Figure 11-4**. Yes ___ No ___

If Yes, go to step 6.

If No, there is another electrical problem in the vehicle. Look for a defective gauge or open or disconnected wires.

Figure 11-2. This gauge reads zero oil pressure at all times. The engine, however, does have oil pressure.

Figure 11-3. Disconnect the pressure sensor connector and ground the lead to the temperature gauge. It is best to ground the sensor connector lead through a test light to avoid damaging the circuit.

Figure 11-4. The gauge has moved to the high pressure side. This indicates that the gauge is operating properly.

☐ 6. Check the switch or sensor with an ohmmeter or special sensor tester.

Is the switch or sensor within specifications? Yes ___ No ___

If Yes, repeat the above steps until the problem is isolated.

If No, replace the switch or sensor and recheck gauge operation.

Switch or Sensor Connected to ECM or Other Electronic Module

☐ 1. Obtain the proper scan tool and related service literature.

Type of scan tool:

_____

☐ 2. Ensure that the ignition switch is in the *Off* position.

☐ 3. Attach the scan tool to the diagnostic connector. If necessary, attach the scan tool power lead to the accessory power outlet or battery.

☐ 4. Ensure that the scan tool is working properly. If the scan tool does not appear to be working, locate and correct any problems before proceeding.

☐ 5. Enter vehicle information as needed to program the scan tool. OBD II scan tools can read needed information from the vehicle computer.

☐ 6. Turn the ignition switch to the *On* position.

☐ 7. Use the scan tool to access the needed module(s) and check for trouble codes.

Are any codes found? Yes ___ No ___

If Yes, list the codes in the spaces provided:

Code   **Defect**

_____   _____

_____   _____

_____   _____

_____   _____

_____   _____

Name _____

☐ 8. Turn the ignition switch to the *Off* position.

☐ 9. Based on the scan tool information, make further checks to locate the defect.

Is the switch or sensor defective? Yes ___ No ___

If Yes, replace the switch or sensor and recheck gauge operation.

If No, there is another electrical problem in the vehicle. Consult your instructor before making further tests.

Remove and Replace Switch or Sensor

☐ 1. Ensure that the ignition switch is in the *Off* position or remove the battery negative cable as directed by the manufacturer.

☐ 2. Remove the switch or sensor electrical connector.

☐ 3. Unscrew the switch or sensor from the attaching part.

☐ 4. Compare the old and new switch or sensors.

Do the threads and electrical connectors match? Yes ___ No ___

If No, what should you do next?

_____

☐ 5. Apply sealer to the switch or sensor threads, if applicable.

☐ 6. Thread the switch or sensor into place and tighten it to the proper torque.

☐ 7. Reinstall the electrical connector.

☐ 8. If necessary, reinstall the battery negative cable.

☐ 9. Start the engine and check sensor operation.

Job Wrap-Up

☐ 1. Clean the work area and return any equipment to storage.

☐ 2. Did you encounter any problems during this procedure? Yes ___ No ___

If Yes, describe the problems:

_____

_____

What did you do to correct the problems?

_____

_____

☐ 3. Have your instructor check your work and sign this job sheet.

Performance Evaluation—Instructor Use Only

Did the student complete the job in the time allotted? Yes ___ No ___

If No, which steps were not completed? _____

How would you rate this student's overall performance on this job?_____

5–Excellent, 4–Good, 3–Satisfactory, 2–Unsatisfactory, 1–Poor

Comments: _____

_____

_____

INSTRUCTOR'S SIGNATURE_____

Project 5

Diagnosing Engine Problems

Introduction

Underneath all of the electronic devices on a modern engine are mechanical parts that would be recognized by a technician from 100 years ago. Before assuming that a problem is in one of the high-tech areas of the vehicle, it is often necessary to use one of the tests covered in this project to eliminate the engine's internal parts as the source of problems.

In the following jobs, you will test engine components and interpret test results. You will perform vacuum and power balance tests in Job 12. In Job 13, you will test engine compression and cylinder leakage. In Job 14, you will check engine oil pressure. You will perform basic engine diagnosis in Job 15.

Project 5 Jobs

- Job 12—Perform a Vacuum Test and a Power Balance Test
- Job 13—Perform a Compression Test and a Cylinder Leakage Test
- Job 14—Perform an Oil Pressure Test
- Job 15—Perform Basic Engine Diagnosis

Tools and Materials

The following list contains the tools and materials that may be needed to complete the jobs in this project. The items used will depend on the make and model of the vehicle being serviced.

- Vehicle in need of service.
- Applicable service information.
- Oil filter wrench.
- Oil drain pan.
- Oil filter.
- Correct type and grade of oil.
- Leak detection equipment.
- Compression gauge.
- Vacuum gauge.
- Scan tool.
- Scan tool operating instructions.

- Shop towels.
- Hand tools.
- Safety glasses and other protective equipment.

Safety Notice

Before performing these jobs, review all pertinent safety information in the text and review safety information with your instructor.

Project 5:   Job 12—Perform a Vacuum Test and a Power Balance Test

After completing this job, you will be able to perform a vacuum test and a power balance test as part of the diagnostic process.

Instructions

As you read the job instructions, answer the questions and perform the tasks. Record your answers using complete sentences. Consult the proper service literature and ask your instructor for help as needed.

> **⚠ Warning:** Before performing this job, review all pertinent safety information in the text and discuss safety procedures with your instructor.

Procedures

☐ 1. Obtain a vehicle to be used in this job. Your instructor may direct you to perform this job on a shop vehicle or engine.

☐ 2. Gather the tools needed to perform the following job. Refer to the tools and materials list at the beginning of the project.

Engine Vacuum Test

☐ 1. Attach a vacuum gauge to the engine. The easiest way to do this is to remove an engine vacuum line and attach the vacuum gauge hose. If a vacuum line cannot be removed or if removing any hose would affect engine operation, the gauge should be connected to the vacuum circuit without interrupting it. This can be accomplished by removing one of the engine's vacuum lines, inserting a length of vacuum hose with a T fitting, and then attaching the vacuum gauge hose to the open nipple on the fitting. It can also be accomplished by removing a fitting from the intake manifold and temporarily installing a hose fitting that allows the gauge to be connected between the vacuum line and the manifold.

☐ 2. Start the engine and allow it to idle.

☐ 3. Refer to the chart in **Figure 12-1** to diagnose engine problems. If necessary, increase engine speed to make further checks.

What conclusions can you make from reading the vacuum gauge?

_____

_____

_____

_____

_____

☐ 4. Turn off the engine.

☐ 5. Remove the vacuum gauge and reattach vacuum hoses or fittings as necessary. If you used a T fitting to attach the vacuum gauge hose, remove the T fitting and reconnect the vacuum line.

Vacuum Gauge Readings

Note: White needle indicates steady vacuum. Red needle indicates fluctuating vacuum.

Needle steady and within specifications.

Cause: Normal vacuum at idle.

Needle very low and steady.

Cause: Vacuum or intake manifold leak.

Needle normal at idle, but fluctuates as engine speed is increased.

Cause: Weak valve spring.

Needle jumps to almost zero when throttle is opened and comes back to just over normal vacuum when closed.

Cause: Normal acceleration and deceleration reading.

Needle slowly drops from normal as engine speed is increased.

Cause: Restricted exhaust (compare at idle and 2500 rpm).

Needle steady, but low at idle.

Cause: Improper valve or ignition timing.

Needle has small pulsation at idle.

Cause: Insufficient spark plug gap.

Needle occasionally makes a sharp fast drop.

Cause: Sticking valve.

Needle regularly drops 4 to 8 inches.

Cause: Blown head gasket or excessive block-to-head clearance.

Needle slowly drifts back and forth.

Cause: Improper air-fuel mixture.

Needle drops regularly; may become steady as engine speed is increased.

Cause: Burned valve, worn valve guide, insufficient tappet clearance.

Needle drops to zero when engine is accelerated and snaps back to higher than normal on deceleration.

Cause: Worn piston rings or diluted oil.

Figure 12-1. Compare the vacuum gauge readings for the engine you are testing with the readings shown here.

Name _____

Power Balance Test

Note: Some testers can measure the amount of power being produced by each engine cylinder without shorting the cylinders. Most of these testers will display cylinder power balance with a bar graph as shown in **Figure 12-2**. This type of tester should be used if available, as it is less likely to damage the catalytic converter.

☐ 1. Attach a power balance testing device. This can be a scan tool or engine analyzer with the capability of shutting down the ignition or fuel injector on individual cylinders. Dedicated power balance testers are available, or individual cylinders can be disabled by shorting secondary wires.

☐ 2. Start the engine and set the engine speed to fast idle before beginning the test.

☐ 3. Kill (disable) each cylinder in turn and record the engine speed as each cylinder is disabled.

Cylinder #1:_____ rpm.   Cylinder #2: _____ rpm.

Cylinder #3:_____ rpm.   Cylinder #4: _____ rpm.

Cylinder #5:_____ rpm.   Cylinder #6: _____ rpm.

Cylinder #7:_____ rpm.   Cylinder #8: _____ rpm.

Cylinder #9: _____ rpm.   Cylinder #10: _____ rpm.

Cylinder #11: _____ rpm.   Cylinder #12: _____ rpm.

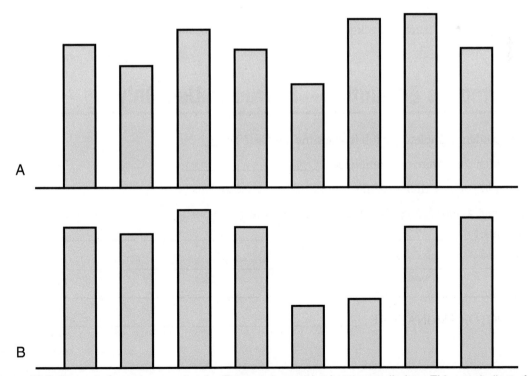

Figure 12-2. Power balance bar graphs. A—Power output varies between cylinders. This may indicate fuel mixture problems, a vacuum leak, or engine wear. This may be a normal reading on some engines. B—When two adjacent cylinders are low, the head gasket may be damaged or the distributor cap (if used) may be carbon tracked.

☐ 4. Return the engine to its normal idle speed and turn it off.

☐ 5. Compare the rpm drops for all cylinders.

Did the rpm fail to drop when any cylinder was disabled? Yes ___ No ___

If Yes, what was the number of the cylinder(s) that did not drop? _____

What do you think could cause the readings you observed?

_____

_____

_____

_____

☐ 6. Remove the test equipment leads from the engine.

Job Wrap-Up

☐ 1. Clean the work area and return any equipment to storage.

☐ 2. Did you encounter any problems during this procedure? Yes ___ No ___

If Yes, describe the problems:

_____

_____

What did you do to correct the problems?

_____

_____

☐ 3. Have your instructor check your work and sign this job sheet.

Performance Evaluation—Instructor Use Only

Did the student complete the job in the time allotted? Yes ___ No ___

If No, which steps were not completed? _____

How would you rate this student's overall performance on this job?_____

5–Excellent, 4–Good, 3–Satisfactory, 2–Unsatisfactory, 1–Poor

Comments: _____

_____

_____

INSTRUCTOR'S SIGNATURE_____

Project 5: Job 13—Perform a Compression Test and a Cylinder Leakage Test

After completing this job, you will be able to perform a compression test and a cylinder leakage test as part of the diagnostic process.

Instructions

As you read the job instructions, answer the questions and perform the tasks. Record your answers using complete sentences. Consult the proper service literature and ask your instructor for help as needed.

Warning: Before performing this job, review all pertinent safety information in the text and discuss safety procedures with your instructor.

Procedures

☐ 1. Obtain a vehicle to be used in this job. Your instructor may direct you to perform this job on a shop vehicle or engine.

☐ 2. Gather the tools needed to perform the following job. Refer to the tools and materials list at the beginning of the project.

Static Compression Test

☐ 1. Remove all spark plugs.

☐ 2. Disable the ignition and fuel systems by either of the following methods.

- **Ignition system:** ground the coil wire or remove the ignition fuse.
- **Fuel system:** remove the fuel pump relay or relay control fuse.

Note: It is not necessary to disable the fuel system on engines with carburetors.

☐ 3. Block the throttle valve in the open position.

☐ 4. Install the compression tester in first spark plug opening.

☐ 5. Crank the engine through four compression strokes. Readings should be something like those shown in **Figure 13-1**.

Record the reading: _____

☐ 6. Repeat steps 4 and 5 for all other engine cylinders.

Cylinder #1:_____	Cylinder #2: _____
Cylinder #3:_____	Cylinder #4: _____
Cylinder #5:_____	Cylinder #6: _____
Cylinder #7:_____	Cylinder #8: _____
Cylinder #9: _____	Cylinder #10: _____
Cylinder #11:_____	Cylinder #12: _____

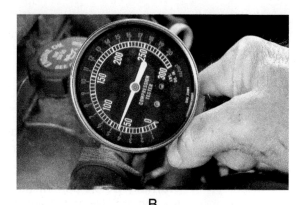

A   B

Figure 13-1. Compression tests can reveal a good deal about the engine's mechanical condition. A—Compression readings should be within 20 percent of the engine manufacturer's specifications. B—A low compression reading indicates worn rings or a burned valve.

☐ 7. Compare the compression readings for all cylinders.

Is the compression excessively low or high on any cylinder(s)? Yes ____ No ____

If Yes, which cylinders have abnormal readings?

_____

What do you think could cause the readings that you observed? Refer to **Figure 13-2** for information about diagnosing compression problems.

_____

_____

_____

_____

☐ 8. If any cylinder had a low compression reading, perform a wet test. Pour approximately one teaspoon (one milliliter) of engine oil into the cylinder and retest the compression.

Did the compression improve? Yes ____ No ____

What is a possible cause?

_____

_____

_____

☐ 9. Return the throttle valve to the closed position and replace the fuel pump relay or relay control fuse if it was removed.

☐ 10. Reinstall the spark plugs and remove the test equipment leads from the engine.

Running Compression Test

☐ 1. Remove the spark plug of the cylinder to be tested. If the spark plugs were removed for the cranking compression test, reinstall them, except the plug of the cylinder to be tested.

☐ 2. Install the compression tester in the spark plug hole.

☐ 3. Start the engine.

☐ 4. Compare the compression reading at idle with the static compression reading.

Is the compression approximately 50% of the static compression reading? Yes ____ No ____

Name _____

Compression Gauge Readings		
Compression Test Results	**Cause**	**Wet Test Results**
All cylinders at normal pressure (no more than 15% difference between cylinders)	Engine is in good shape, no problems.	No wet test needed.
All cylinders low (more than 20% below specifications)	Burned valve or valve seat, blown head gasket, worn rings or cylinder, valves misadjusted, jumped timing chain or belt, physical damage to engine.	If compression increases, cylinder or rings are worn. No increase, problem caused by valve train. Near zero compression caused by engine damage.
One or more cylinders low (more than 20% difference)	Burned valve, valve seat, damage or wear on affected cylinder(s).	If compression increases, cylinder or rings are worn. No increase, problem caused by valve train. Near zero compression caused by engine damage.
Two adjacent cylinders low (more than 20% difference)	Blown head gasket, cracked block or head.	Little or no increase in pressure.
Compression high (more than 20% difference)	Carbon build-up in cylinder.	Do not wet test for high compression.

Figure 13-2. The causes of the these compression readings apply to any engine. Consult the manufacturer's service literature for any special problem.

☐ 5. Quickly snap the throttle open and closed.

Does compression rise to about 80% of the static compression reading? Yes ___ No ___

☐ 6. Repeat steps 4 and 5 for all other engine cylinders.

Note: Reinstall each plug before moving to the next cylinder. Leaving out any plug other than the plug to be tested will affect readings.

Cylinder #1:_____   Cylinder #2: _____

Cylinder #3:_____   Cylinder #4: _____

Cylinder #5:_____   Cylinder #6: _____

Cylinder #7:_____   Cylinder #8: _____

Cylinder #9: _____   Cylinder #10: _____

Cylinder #11:_____   Cylinder #12: _____

☐ 7. Compare the compression readings for all cylinders.

Is the running compression excessively low or high on any cylinder(s)? Yes ___ No ___

If Yes, which cylinders have abnormal readings?

_____

What do you think could cause the readings that you observed? Possible causes include worn camshaft lobes, excessive carbon deposits on the valves, and worn rings.

_____

_____

_____

☐ 8. Ensure that all plugs have been properly reinstalled and torqued.

☐ 9. Remove all test equipment.

Compression Test Using Pressure Transducer and Scope—Optional Task

1. Remove the spark plug from the cylinder to be tested.

> **Note:** Some transducer procedures call for removing <u>all</u> spark plugs to perform Steps 2 through 6.

2. Install a pressure transducer of the correct pressure range in the cylinder to be tested. Use hoses as necessary to connect the transducer to the spark plug opening. Hoses used should *not* contain a Schrader valve.

3. Make the necessary electrical connections between the transducer and a scope capable of reading transducer output.

4. Set the scope to read engine compression waveforms.

5. Disable the ignition.

6. Crank the engine while reading the scope.

7. Observe the scope pattern.

   Does the pattern shape indicate a cylinder compression problem? Yes ___ No ___
   If Yes, explain.

   _____

   _____

   _____

8. Repeat steps 1 through 7 for each of the remaining cylinders to confirm that the problem is isolated to the first cylinder tested.

9. Reinstall the transducer in the first spark plug opening.

10. Reinstall the other spark plugs as necessary and restore ignition system operation.

11. Ground the disconnected plug wire if necessary.

12. Start the engine and observe the scope pattern.

    Can you detect a problem by the shape of the pattern? Yes ___ No ___
    If Yes, explain.

    _____

    _____

    _____

13. Repeat steps 9 through 12 for each of the remaining cylinders to confirm that the problem is isolated to the first cylinder tested.

    Has the first cylinder problem been confirmed? Yes ___ No ___
    Explain your answer.

    _____

    _____

    _____

14. Reinstall the spark plug(s), as necessary.

Project 5: Job 13 (continued)

Cylinder Leakage Test

Note: A cylinder leakage test is usually performed when a compression test indicates low compression on a cylinder. Your instructor may direct you to perform this test on a randomly selected cylinder in good condition.

☐   1. Disable the ignition system to prevent accidental starting.

☐   2. Attach a shop air hose to the leak tester.

☐   3. Adjust the tester pressure to the recommended setting. This is usually about 5–10 psi (35–70 kPa).
     Manufacturer's pressure setting: _____ psi or kPa (circle one).

☐   4. Remove the spark plug from the suspect cylinder.

☐   5. Bring the suspect cylinder to the top of its compression stroke by feeling for compression as the piston comes up. Some technicians use a whistle to indicate when the compression stroke is occurring.

☐   6. Install the leak tester hose in the spark plug opening.

☐   7. Open the valve allowing regulated pressure into the cylinder.

☐   8. Observe the pressure. It should be at or near the regulated pressure.
     Pressure reading: _____ psi or kPa (circle one).
     Does this pressure match the regulated pressure? Yes ___ No ___
     If No, what is a possible cause?

     _____

     _____

     _____

     _____

☐   9. If the pressure is low, refer to the chart in **Figure 13-3**.
     After consulting the chart, list the possible engine problem:

     _____

     _____

     _____

     _____

☐ 10. Remove the tester hose and reinstall the spark plug.

☐ 11. Repeat steps 4 through 10 on all suspect cylinders.

☐ 12. Analyze the readings of all tested cylinders.
     What conclusions can you make?

     _____

     _____

     _____

☐ 13. Remove the shop air hose from the tester.

Job Wrap-Up

☐   1. Clean the work area and return any equipment to storage.

Cylinder Leakage Test Results	
Condition	**Possible Causes**
No air escapes from any of the cylinders.	Normal condition, no leakage.
Air escapes from carburetor or throttle body.	Intake valve not seated or damaged. Incorrect valve timing. Possible jumped timing chain or belt. Broken or damaged valve train part.
Air escapes from tailpipe.	Exhaust valve not seated or is damaged. Incorrect valve timing. Broken or damaged valve train part.
Air escapes from dipstick tube or oil fill opening.	Worn piston rings. Worn cylinder walls. Damaged piston. Blown head gasket.
Air escapes from adjacent cylinder.	Blown head gasket. Cracked head or block.
Air bubbles in radiator coolant.	Blown head gasket. Cracked head or block.
Air heard around outside of cylinder.	Cracked or warped head or block. Blown head gasket.

Figure 13-3. The engine cylinder is supposed to be almost air tight at the top of its compression stroke. Air escaping anywhere is caused by a defect.

□ 2. Did you encounter any problems during this procedure? Yes ___ No ___
If Yes, describe the problems:

_____

_____

What did you do to correct the problems?

_____

_____

□ 3. Have your instructor check your work and sign this job sheet.

Performance Evaluation—Instructor Use Only

Did the student complete the job in the time allotted? Yes ___ No ___

If No, which steps were not completed? _____

How would you rate this student's overall performance on this job?_____

5–Excellent, 4–Good, 3–Satisfactory, 2–Unsatisfactory, 1–Poor

Comments: _____

_____

_____

INSTRUCTOR'S SIGNATURE_____

Name _____

Date _____ Class _____

After completing this job, you will be able to perform an oil pressure test as part of the diagnostic process.

Instructions

As you read the job instructions, answer the questions and perform the tasks. Record your answers using complete sentences. Consult the proper service literature and ask your instructor for help as needed.

 Warning: Before performing this job, review all pertinent safety information in the text and discuss safety procedures with your instructor.

Procedures

☐ 1. Obtain a vehicle to be used in this job. Your instructor may direct you to perform this job on a shop vehicle or engine.

☐ 2. Gather the tools needed to perform the following job. Refer to the tools and materials list at the beginning of the project.

☐ 3. Locate the oil pressure sender and remove it.

☐ 4. Install an oil pressure gauge in the sender opening.

Caution: Position the hose on the oil pressure gauge away from moving parts and the exhaust system.

☐ 5. Start the engine.

☐ 6. Measure the oil pressure at idle, **Figure 14-1**.

Pressure: _____ psi or kPa (circle one).

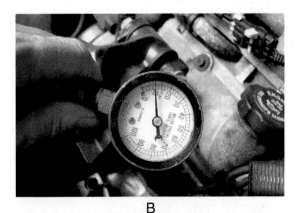

A   B

Figure 14-1. A—This reading shows 30 psi (about 210 kPa) at idle, which is an acceptable reading. B—This reading is less than 10 psi (about 70 kPa). While this is probably not low enough to turn on the oil light, it indicates a developing problem.

⚠️ **Warning:** If the oil pressure is zero, stop the engine immediately and determine the cause.

☐ 7. Raise the engine speed to 2500 rpm and measure the oil pressure.
Pressure: _____ psi or kPa (circle one).

☐ 8. Compare the pressure readings to the manufacturer's specifications.
What conclusions can you make?

_____

_____

_____

☐ 9. Shut off the vehicle. Remove the gauge from the pressure sender opening.

☐ 10. Reinstall the pressure sender.

Job Wrap-Up

☐ 1. Clean the work area and return any equipment to storage.

☐ 2. Did you encounter any problems during this procedure? Yes ___ No ___
If Yes, describe the problems:

_____

_____

What did you do to correct the problems?

_____

_____

☐ 3. Have your instructor check your work and sign this job sheet.

Performance Evaluation—Instructor Use Only

Did the student complete the job in the time allotted? Yes ___ No ___

If No, which steps were not completed? _____

How would you rate this student's overall performance on this job?_____

5–Excellent, 4–Good, 3–Satisfactory, 2–Unsatisfactory, 1–Poor

Comments: _____

_____

_____

INSTRUCTOR'S SIGNATURE_____

Copyright Goodheart-Willcox Co., Inc.
May not be reproduced or posted to a publicly accessible website

Project 5: Job 15—Perform Basic Engine Diagnosis

After completing this job, you will be able to perform basic engine diagnosis.

Instructions

As you read the job instructions, answer the questions and perform the tasks. Record your answers using complete sentences. Consult the proper service literature and ask your instructor for help as needed.

⚠️ **Warning:** Before performing this job, review all pertinent safety information in the text and discuss safety procedures with your instructor.

Procedures

☐ 1. Obtain an engine to be used in this job. Your instructor may direct you to perform this job on a shop vehicle.
  • Make of engine: _____
  • Number of cylinders: _____
  • Cylinder arrangement (V-type, inline, etc.): _____
  • Cooling system: Liquid ___ Air ___

☐ 2. Gather the tools needed to perform the following tasks. Refer to the tools and materials list at the beginning of the project.

Preliminary Checks

☐ 1. Question the vehicle driver and note which of the following categories the problem falls into. In the following series of questions, you will be asking under what conditions these defects occur. Typical responses would be hot or cold, under load or coasting, in gear or out, at idle or cruising, and other descriptions.

Noises

Light clatter. ___ Under what conditions?

_____

Light knocking. ___ Under what conditions?

_____

Heavy knocking. ___ Under what conditions?

_____

Rattles. ___ Under what conditions?

_____

Whines. ___ Under what conditions?

_____

Vibration

Describe any vibration-related complaints:

_____

_____

_____

Rough idle

Describe unusual idle conditions:

_____

_____

_____

Engine miss

Under what conditions?

_____

_____

_____

Lack of power

Under what conditions?

_____

_____

_____

Exhaust noises or odors

Describe the complaint:

_____

_____

_____

Under what conditions?

_____

_____

_____

Exhaust smoke

Black ___

Blue ___

White ___

Under what conditions?

_____

_____

_____

2. Road test the vehicle.

Could the problem be duplicated? Yes ___ No ___

Does your description of the problem agree with the driver's description of the problem?
Yes ___ No ___

Name _____

If No, explain why:

_____

_____

_____

☐ 3. Refer to the appropriate engine service information.

Does the engine service information address the specific problem? Yes ___ No ___

If Yes, briefly describe the information:

_____

_____

_____

Does the service information provide clues to the cause of the problem? Yes ___ No ___

If Yes, briefly describe the information:

_____

_____

_____

☐ 4. Check for obvious problems by making a visual inspection of the engine compartment with the engine running and not running.

Leaks

Oil. ___ Describe the location:

_____

Coolant. ___ Describe the location:

_____

Vacuum. ___ Describe the location:

_____

Exhaust. ___ Describe the location:

_____

Damaged parts

Describe any damaged parts:

_____

_____

_____

Signs of poor maintenance or lack of service

Describe any problems:

_____

_____

_____

Other problems

Describe:

_____

_____

_____

Note: In cases where an obvious problem is located before all steps are completed, your instructor may approve skipping some of the steps.

Determine the Cause of the Problem

☐ 1. Check engine mechanical systems.

Manifold vacuum

Describe any problems:

_____

_____

_____

Cylinder compression

Cylinder #1:_____   Cylinder #2: _____

Cylinder #3:_____   Cylinder #4: _____

Cylinder #5:_____   Cylinder #6: _____

Cylinder #7:_____   Cylinder #8: _____

Cylinder #9: _____   Cylinder #10: _____

Cylinder #11:_____   Cylinder #12: _____

Engine and transmission/transaxle mounts

Describe the location of any broken or damaged mounts:

_____

_____

_____

Other problems

Describe any other problems detected:

_____

_____

_____

☐ 2. Check engine electrical systems.

Starting system

Describe any problems found:

_____

_____

_____

Charging system

Describe any problems found:

_____

_____

_____

Name _____

Ignition system

Describe any problems found:

_____

_____

_____

☐ 3. Check engine fuel system.

Fuel pressure

Describe any problems found:

_____

_____

_____

Injector waveforms

Describe any problems found:

_____

_____

_____

Fuel filter

Describe any problems found:

_____

_____

_____

☐ 4. Check engine computer control system.

Trouble codes

List any trouble codes retrieved:

_____

_____

_____

Out-of-specification readings

List any readings that are out of specification:

_____

_____

_____

Other scan tool information

List any other important information:

_____

_____

_____

☐ 5. Check engine-related accessories.

Air conditioning compressor

List any problems detected:

_____

_____

_____

Power steering pump

List any problems detected:

_____

_____

_____

Power brake booster

List any problems detected:

_____

_____

_____

☐ 6. Check exhaust system.

Leaks

Describe:

_____

_____

_____

Rattles

Describe:

_____

_____

_____

Restrictions

Describe:

_____

_____

_____

☐ 7. Check drive train systems.

Transmission/clutch

List any abnormal conditions or readings that were not within specifications:

_____

_____

_____

Name _____

Torque converter/lockup clutch

List any abnormal conditions or readings that were not within specifications:

_____

_____

_____

☐ 8. Review the information you have collected.

Do you think the conditions you identified could be the cause(s) of the problem?
Yes ___ No ___

Explain your answer:

_____

_____

_____

☐ 9. Eliminate causes of the problem by checking components that could cause the abnormal conditions found.

List any defective components or systems that you located:

_____

_____

Do you think these defects could be the cause of the original problem? Yes ___ No ___

Explain your answer:

_____

_____

☐ 10. Isolate and recheck possible causes of the problem.

Did the rechecking procedure reveal any new problems or establish that suspected components were in fact good? Yes ___ No ___

If there were any differences with the conclusions in step 8, what was the reason?

_____

_____

☐ 11. Correct the defect by making necessary repairs or adjustments.

Briefly describe the services performed:

_____

_____

_____

☐ 12. Recheck system operation by performing either or both of the following:

Make checks using test equipment. ___

Road test the vehicle. ___

Did the services in step 11 correct the problem? Yes ___ No ___

If No, what steps should you take now?

_____

_____

_____

Job Wrap-Up

☐ 1. Clean the work area and return any equipment to storage.

☐ 2. Did you encounter any problems during this procedure? Yes ___ No ___

If Yes, describe the problems:

_____

_____

What did you do to correct the problems?

_____

_____

☐ 3. Have your instructor check your work and sign this job sheet.

Performance Evaluation—Instructor Use Only

Did the student complete the job in the time allotted? Yes ___ No ___

If No, which steps were not completed? _____

How would you rate this student's overall performance on this job?_____

5–Excellent, 4–Good, 3–Satisfactory, 2–Unsatisfactory, 1–Poor

Comments: _____

_____

_____

INSTRUCTOR'S SIGNATURE_____

Project 6

Removing and Disassembling an Engine

Introduction

While engine designs vary greatly between manufacturers, the general steps for removal are similar. The most important part of the job is to make sure that the lifting fixtures are safely and properly installed. Everything that connects the engine to the body, such as hoses, wires, and cables, must be removed before lifting the engine from the vehicle.

In Job 16, you will remove an engine from a vehicle. Once the engine is removed from the vehicle, it can be disassembled for repair or overhaul. In Job 17, you will completely disassemble an engine.

Project 6 Jobs

- Job 16—Remove an Engine
- Job 17—Disassemble an Engine

Tools and Materials

The following list contains the tools and materials that may be needed to complete the jobs in this project. The items used will depend on the make and model of the vehicle being serviced.

- Vehicle with an engine in need of removal and overhaul.
- Engine lift.
- Engine lifting hook and chain assembly.
- Engine holding fixture.
- Applicable service information.
- Hand tools.
- Air-powered tools.
- Safety glasses and other protective equipment.

Safety Notice

Before performing these jobs, review all pertinent safety information in the text and review safety information with your instructor.

Notes

Project 6:   Job 16—Remove an Engine

After completing this job, you will be able to prepare an engine for removal, properly attach a lifting fixture, and remove the engine from the vehicle.

Instructions

As you read the job instructions, answer the questions and perform the tasks. Record your answers using complete sentences. Consult the proper service literature and ask your instructor for help as needed.

> ⚠️ **Warning:** Before performing this job, review all pertinent safety information in the text and discuss safety procedures with your instructor.

Procedures

> **Note:** Since most engines are removed through the top of the engine compartment, this procedure concentrates on top removal. If the engine is removed from the bottom of the vehicle, substitute the manufacturer's removal procedures at all steps referring to top removal and installation.

☐ 1. Obtain a vehicle to be used in this job. Your instructor may direct you to perform this job on a shop vehicle.

Briefly describe the engine to be used for this job:

_____

☐ 2. Gather the tools needed to perform the following steps. Refer to the tools and materials list at the beginning of the project.

Prepare the Engine for Removal

☐ 1. Scribe around the hood hinges so they can be reinstalled in the same position. Then, remove the hood and set it aside in a place where it will not be damaged.

☐ 2. Disconnect the battery negative cable.

☐ 3. Depressurize the fuel system.

   Type of fuel system

   • Multipoint fuel injection. ___

   • Central fuel injection. ___

   • Carburetor. ___

☐ 4. Drain the engine coolant.

> **Note:** If the engine has an auxiliary oil cooler, drain the oil and remove the cooler lines at this time.

☐ 5. Remove the upper and lower radiator hoses.

☐   6. Remove the heater hoses.

☐   7. Remove any engine harness connectors at the firewall or body and any electrical cables or ground straps between the body and engine. Mark them for reinstallation.

☐   8. Remove any belts as needed.

☐   9. Remove the mounting bolts from the power steering pump (if used) and tie the pump to the body, away from the engine.

☐ 10. Remove the mounting bolts from the air conditioning compressor (if used) and tie the compressor to the body, away from the engine.

> **Note:** Usually the alternator and air pump (when used) can be left on the engine during removal. You may, however, want to remove them at this time to prevent possible damage.

☐ 11. Remove the air cleaner assembly or the air inlet ducts to the throttle body.

☐ 12. Remove the throttle cable and the transmission and cruise control cables, if used.

☐ 13. Remove the fuel inlet and return lines.

☐ 14. Remove all vacuum hoses from the intake manifold and mark them for reinstallation.

> **Note:** To perform steps 15 through 19, the vehicle must be raised. Raise the vehicle in a safe manner to gain access to the underside.

☐ 15. From underneath the vehicle, disconnect the exhaust system.

☐ 16. From underneath the vehicle, remove any brackets holding the engine to the transmission or transaxle.

☐ 17. Remove the flywheel cover.

☐ 18. Remove the starter wiring and the starter.

☐ 19. If the vehicle has an automatic transmission or transaxle, mark the relative positions of the engine flywheel and torque converter. Then, remove the flywheel-to-torque converter fasteners.

> **Note:** If the vehicle has a manual transmission, do not remove the bolts holding the pressure plate to the flywheel. The clutch assembly can be removed with the engine.

Remove the Engine

☐   1. Lower the vehicle and install an engine lifting bracket or other lifting fixture on the engine. **Figure 16-1** shows the use of a bracket originally used to install the engine in the vehicle at the factory.

Describe how you installed the lifting device:

_____

_____

Name_____

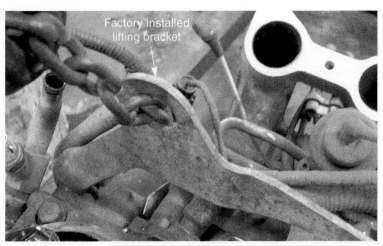

Figure 16-1. This bracket was installed on the engine at the factory and can be used to remove and replace the engine in the field.

 Warning: The lifting devices must be installed correctly to avoid personal injury or damage to the vehicle. Consult your instructor before using the lifting device to raise the engine. **Figure 16-2** shows the placement of the lifting chain on a 6-cylinder engine.

☐ 2. Connect the lifting fixture to an engine hoist.

☐ 3. Raise the engine to remove the tension on the engine mounts.

☐ 4. Remove the engine mount fasteners and brackets as necessary.

☐ 5. Support the transmission or transaxle.

Describe how you supported the transmission or transaxle:

_____

_____

☐ 6. Remove the fasteners holding the transmission or transaxle to the engine.

Figure 16-2. The placement of the lifting chain used to remove an inline 6-cylinder engine from a pickup truck is shown here.

☐ 7. Separate the engine and transmission or transaxle.
☐ 8. Raise the engine and remove it from the vehicle.

> **Caution:** While raising the engine, watch carefully for any wires or hoses that you may have forgotten to remove.

☐ 9. Lower the engine as soon as it clears the vehicle and install it on an engine-holding fixture.

Job Wrap-Up

☐ 1. Clean the work area and return any equipment to storage.
☐ 2. Did you encounter any problems during this procedure? Yes ___ No ___
     If Yes, describe the problems:

     _____

     _____

     What did you do to correct the problems?

     _____

     _____

☐ 3. Have your instructor check your work and sign this job sheet.

Performance Evaluation—Instructor Use Only

Did the student complete the job in the time allotted? Yes ___ No ___

If No, which steps were not completed? _____

How would you rate this student's overall performance on this job?_____

5–Excellent, 4–Good, 3–Satisfactory, 2–Unsatisfactory, 1–Poor

Comments: _____

_____

_____

INSTRUCTOR'S SIGNATURE_____

Project 6: Job 17—Disassemble an Engine

After completing this job, you will be able to properly disassemble an engine.

Instructions

As you read the job instructions, answer the questions and perform the tasks. Record your answers using complete sentences. Consult the proper service literature and ask your instructor for help as needed.

> **Warning:** Before performing this job, review all pertinent safety information in the text and discuss safety procedures with your instructor.

Procedures

☐ 1. Obtain an engine to be used in this job. Your instructor may direct you to perform this job on a shop engine.
- Make of engine: _____
- Number of cylinders: _____
- Cylinder arrangement (V-type, inline, etc.): _____
- Cooling system: Liquid ____ Air ____

☐ 2. Gather the tools needed to perform the following tasks. Refer to the tools and materials list at the beginning of the project.

> **Note:** If the clutch assembly is installed on the flywheel, remove it before proceeding with the disassembly.

Begin Disassembly

☐ 1. Remove the engine flywheel.
☐ 2. Install the engine on an engine stand.
☐ 3. Drain the oil, if not already done, and remove the oil filter.
☐ 4. Remove all accessory parts, noting their position for reinstallation:
- Engine mount brackets.
- Accessory attaching brackets.
- Belt tensioner bracket, if used.
- Turbocharger or supercharger, if used.
- Dipstick and tube.
- Ignition module, coils, and plug wires.

☐ 5. Remove the distributor, if used.

Project 6: Job 17 (continued)

☐ 6. Remove the valve cover(s). If the ignition coils are installed on the valve cover, remove the coils before removing the cover.

☐ 7. Remove the upper intake manifold or plenum.

☐ 8. Remove the lower intake manifold, if used.

☐ 9. Remove the thermostat housing if it is not part of the intake manifold.

☐ 10. Remove the exhaust crossover pipe, if applicable.

☐ 11. Remove the exhaust manifold(s).

☐ 12. Remove the oil filter adapter, if used.

☐ 13. Mark the rocker arms or rocker arm shaft(s) so that all parts can be installed in their original position, then remove the rocker arms and/or shaft(s).

> **Note:** If the engine has an overhead camshaft, it is often easier to leave the rocker arms in place until the head is disassembled.

☐ 14. Remove the push rods, if applicable.

☐ 15. Remove the valve lifters or lash adjusters as applicable.

☐ 16. If the engine has a mechanical fuel pump, remove it.

☐ 17. Remove the coolant pump.

☐ 18. Remove the vibration damper (crankshaft balancer), any attached pulleys, and the crankshaft key. Inspect the vibration damper and obtain a replacement if needed.

> **Note:** Some vibration dampers slide from the crankshaft when the bolt is removed from the crankshaft. Others must be removed with a puller. Consult the proper service literature to determine the removal method to be used.

☐ 19. Remove the timing cover.

☐ 20. Remove the oil pump and drive.

☐ 21. Remove the timing gears or sprockets and the related chain or belt. A puller may be needed to remove the timing gear from the crankshaft. See **Figure 17-1**.

☐ 22. If the camshaft is installed in the block, remove the camshaft.

☐ 23. If the engine contains one or more chain-driven balance shafts, remove the chain(s) now.

☐ 24. Rotate the engine on the stand to gain access to the oil pan. Remove the oil pan.

Remove the Cylinder Head(s)

☐ 1. Rotate the engine on the stand to gain access to the cylinder head(s).

☐ 2. Loosen and remove the cylinder head bolts.

> **Note:** On some overhead cam engines, it may be necessary to remove the camshaft(s) and rocker arm shaft(s) to reach some of the head bolts. Removal is covered in more detail in Job 24.

Project 6: Job 17 *(continued)*

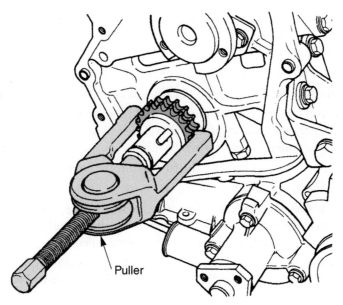

Figure 17-1. A puller may be needed to remove the crankshaft gear. (Chrysler)

☐   3. Gently pry between the head and the block to loosen the gasket, then remove the head.

☐   4. Inspect the head gasket for signs of gasket failure.

     Is there any evidence of gasket failure? Yes ___ No ___

     If Yes, describe:

     _____

     _____

     _____

Remove the Pistons

☐   1. Turn the crankshaft with a breaker bar and socket to position the piston to be removed at the bottom of its cylinder.

☐   2. Check the cylinder for wear or damage. Look for scratches, grooves, and signs of overheating. A shiny surface indicates normal cylinder wear.

☐   3. Move your fingernail from the midpoint of the cylinder wall to the very top of the cylinder wall. If your fingernail hangs up solidly on the ridge formed at the top of the piston ring travel, the cylinder is worn excessively.

     Does the ring ridge indicate excessive wear? Yes ___ No ___

> **Caution:** The ring ridge must be removed before the piston is removed. Forcing the piston over the ring ridge can break the rings and damage the piston grooves and lands.

☐   4. Place shop rags in the cylinder to catch metal chips.

☐   5. Insert the ridge-reaming tool into the cylinder.

☐   6. Adjust the cutters against the ridge.

☐ 7. Turn the reamer with a hand wrench or a ratchet and socket until the ridge is cut flush with the worn part of the cylinder wall. The new reamed surface must blend smoothly with the existing cylinder. Do not undercut the ridge.

☐ 8. Remove the rags and blow out the cylinder to remove metal shavings.

☐ 9. Rotate the engine on the engine stand to gain access to the connecting rod, **Figure 17-2**.

☐ 10. Check that the rod cap and rod are numbered. If they are not numbered, mark them with a punch and hammer or a number punch, if available. Also mark the rod and cap in a way so that the cap can be reinstalled in the original position.

☐ 11. Loosen and remove the nuts holding the rod cap on the connecting rod.

☐ 12. Remove the connecting rod cap.

☐ 13. Check that the piston head has a mark to indicate which direction it should face when reinstalled. If there is no mark, mark the connecting rod to indicate the front of the engine. The pistons must face in the original direction when reinstalled.

☐ 14. Remove the piston from the cylinder by pushing the connecting rod toward the top of the block. If the piston is difficult to remove, lightly tap on the connecting rod with a plastic faced hammer or block of wood.

☐ 15. Repeat steps 1 through 14 to remove all of the pistons. Place all of the pistons in order for reassembly.

☐ 16. Inspect the pistons for scuffed or scratched skirts, damage to the ring grooves and lands, damage to the piston head, and worn piston (wrist) pin bores. These procedures are covered in Job 22.

Remove the Crankshaft

☐ 1. Rotate the engine on the stand to gain access to the main bearing caps.

☐ 2. Mark the crankshaft main bearing caps so that they can be reinstalled in the same position and orientation.

Figure 17-2. The connecting rod nuts can be seen once the oil pan has been removed. (Heli-Coil)

Name _____

☐ 3. If the engine uses a one-piece rear main seal, use a small screwdriver to pry out the seal. Be careful not to damage the main cap or block. Some one-piece seals are installed in a separate housing behind the rear main bearing. It is usually easier to pry out the seal before removing the housing.

☐ 4. Loosen and remove the main bearing cap fasteners.

☐ 5. Remove the main bearing caps from the block.

☐ 6. Lift the crankshaft from the engine block. Store the crankshaft as shown in **Figure 17-3**. This reduces the chance of crankshaft warping.

Note: Crankshaft inspection is covered in Job 18.

☐ 7. If the engine uses a two-piece rear main seal, use a small screwdriver to remove the seal segments from the main cap and the block. Be careful not to scratch the cap or the block.

☐ 8. If necessary, on an aluminum block, remove the cylinder liners using a special removal tool.

Note: Some aluminum engines have non-removable cylinder liners. Check the applicable service literature before attempting to remove the liners.

Figure 17-3. Store the crankshaft standing straight up. Allowing the crankshaft to rest on its side for long periods can cause it to warp.

☐ 9. If the engine uses one or more balance shafts, remove them from the block.

Note: Some engine blocks are made in two or more sections. If necessary, remove the fasteners and disassemble the block.

Job Wrap-Up

☐ 1. Clean the work area and return any equipment to storage.
☐ 2. Did you encounter any problems during this procedure? Yes ___ No ___
If Yes, describe the problems:

_____

_____

What did you do to correct the problems?

_____

_____

☐ 3. Have your instructor check your work and sign this job sheet.

Performance Evaluation—Instructor Use Only

Did the student complete the job in the time allotted? Yes ___ No ___

If No, which steps were not completed? _____

How would you rate this student's overall performance on this job?_____

5–Excellent, 4–Good, 3–Satisfactory, 2–Unsatisfactory, 1–Poor
Comments: _____

_____

_____

INSTRUCTOR'S SIGNATURE_____

Project 7

Performing Bottom End Service

Introduction

The engine block is the foundation of the engine. The pistons in the cylinders transform the energy released in combustion into reciprocal motion, and the connecting rods transfer that motion to the crankshaft. The crankshaft converts the up and down motion of the pistons into rotary motion to drive the wheels. Together, these components are frequently referred to as the engine's bottom end.

While modern engines last longer than their predecessors, vehicles are staying on the road for many more years than previously occurred. Longer vehicle life means that internal engine parts must operate for longer periods and will eventually wear out. Engine block and crankshaft problems must be diagnosed and corrected. These problems can result in loss of compression, oil burning, and noise. Crankshaft and bearing problems cause noises and low oil pressure.

In this project, you will inspect and service the engine's block, crankshaft, pistons, connecting rods, and other bottom end components. You will inspect the block, crankshaft, and bearings in Job 18. In Job 19, you will learn how to repair a variety of damaged threads. You will measure cylinder wear and hone the cylinders in Job 20. You will inspect the connecting rods in Job 21, and inspect the pistons and replace piston rings in Job 22. In Job 23, you will inspect balance shafts, the vibration damper, and the oil pump.

Project 7 Jobs

- Job 18—Inspect the Block, Crankshaft, and Bearings
- Job 19—Repair Damaged Threads
- Job 20—Measure Cylinder Wear and Hone Cylinders
- Job 21—Inspect Connecting Rods
- Job 22—Inspect Pistons and Replace Piston Rings
- Job 23—Inspect Balance Shafts, the Vibration Damper, and the Oil Pump

Tools and Materials

The following list contains the tools and materials that may be needed to complete the jobs in this project. The items used will depend on the make and model of the vehicle being serviced.

- Disassembled engine.
- Applicable service information.
- Ridge reamer.

- Ring expander.
- Inside micrometer.
- Outside micrometer.
- Set of flat feeler gauges.
- Engine oil.
- Cylinder hone.
- Air or electric drill.
- Crack-detection equipment.
- Thread repair tools.
- Thread repair inserts.
- Straightedge.
- Hand tools.
- Air-powered tools.
- Safety glasses and other protective equipment.

Safety Notice

Before performing these jobs, review all pertinent safety information in the text and review safety information with your instructor.

Name_____

Date _____ Class _____

Project 7:   Job 18—Inspect the Block, Crankshaft, and Bearings

After completing this job, you will be able to inspect a block, crankshaft, and bearings.

Instructions

As you read the job instructions, answer the questions and perform the tasks. Record your answers using complete sentences. Consult the proper service literature and ask your instructor for help as needed.

> ⚠ **Warning:** Before performing this job, review all pertinent safety information in the text and discuss safety procedures with your instructor.

Procedures

> **Note:** This job assumes that the engine block has been disassembled. Refer to Job 17 for disassembly procedures.

☐ 1. Obtain an engine to be used in this job. Your instructor may direct you to perform this job on a shop engine.

☐ 2. Identify the engine by listing the following information.

   • Engine maker: _____

   • Number of cylinders: _____

   • Engine displacement: _____

☐ 3. Gather the tools needed to perform the following job. Refer to the tools and materials list at the beginning of the project.

Check the Engine Block for Defects

☐ 1. Check the engine block for obvious defects, **Figure 18-1**.

   • Obvious cracks.

      Are there any obvious cracks? Yes ___ No ___

> **Note:** If you suspect that the block has a crack that cannot be found by visual inspection, it will be necessary to check the block by magnetic or black light methods. Ask your instructor if further crack testing should be performed. Magnetic detection methods cannot be used to check aluminum blocks.

Figure 18-1. Once the engine is disassembled and cleaned, check the block carefully for cracks and other damage.

- Damaged core (freeze) plugs, **Figure 18-2**. These can usually be spotted by streaks caused by leaking coolant. Most technicians prefer to replace the core plugs whenever the engine is overhauled regardless of the condition.

  Are there any damaged core plugs? Yes ___ No ___

- Stripped fastener threads. Some threads can be repaired with special procedures, explained in Job 19.

  Are there any stripped threads? Yes ___ No ___

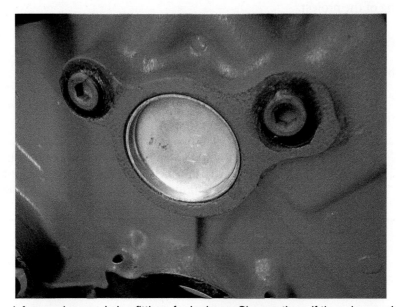

Figure 18-2. Check freeze plugs and pipe fittings for leakage. Change them if there is any sign of leakage. Most technicians routinely change the freeze plugs as part of an engine overhaul.

Name _____

☐ 2. Check the engine block deck (cylinder head surface of the block) for warping where it seals against the head(s). Place a straightedge across the block deck at various angles and attempt to slide different size feeler gauge blades between the straightedge and the block. Acceptable warpage is around 0.003" (0.08 mm) over any 6" (150 mm) surface.

What is the largest blade that will fit between the straightedge and head?

_____

If the head is warped more than the specification, what should be done next?

_____

_____

_____

Inspect the Crankshaft and Bearings

☐ 1. Check the condition of the main bearings and crankshaft journals. **Figure 18-3** shows obvious damage to a block and bearing cap.

Condition(s) observed

Pitting ___ Scratches ___ Ridges ___ Overheating ___ Other (describe):

_____

_____

Describe where the damage was found:

_____

_____

Note: Severe wear on several adjacent main bearings while others have only normal wear indicates that the bearing bore in the block is misaligned or that the crankshaft is bent. Wear on one side of a single connecting rod bearing usually indicates a bent or twisted connecting rod. Refer to Job 21 for connecting rod inspection.

Figure 18-3. This block and bearing cap were severely damaged. Most damage will not be as obvious.

☐ 2. Take the following measurements using the proper micrometer. See **Figure 18-4**.

Connecting rod journal #1

Specified diameter: _____   Measured diameter: _____

Connecting rod journal #2

Specified diameter: _____   Measured diameter: _____

Connecting rod journal #3

Specified diameter: _____   Measured diameter: _____

Connecting rod journal #4

Specified diameter: _____   Measured diameter: _____

Connecting rod journal #5

Specified diameter: _____   Measured diameter: _____

Connecting rod journal #6

Specified diameter: _____   Measured diameter: _____

Connecting rod journal #7

Specified diameter: _____   Measured diameter: _____

Connecting rod journal #8

Specified diameter: _____   Measured diameter: _____

Connecting rod journal #9

Specified diameter: _____   Measured diameter: _____

Connecting rod journal #10

Specified diameter: _____   Measured diameter: _____

Connecting rod journal #11

Specified diameter: _____   Measured diameter: _____

Connecting rod journal #12

Specified diameter: _____   Measured diameter: _____

Main bearing journal #1

Specified diameter: _____   Measured diameter: _____

Main bearing journal #2

Specified diameter: _____   Measured diameter: _____

Main bearing journal #3

Specified diameter: _____   Measured diameter: _____

Main bearing journal #4

Specified diameter: _____   Measured diameter: _____

Main bearing journal #5

Specified diameter: _____   Measured diameter: _____

Main bearing journal #6

Specified diameter: _____   Measured diameter: _____

Main bearing journal #7

Specified diameter: _____   Measured diameter: _____

Name _____

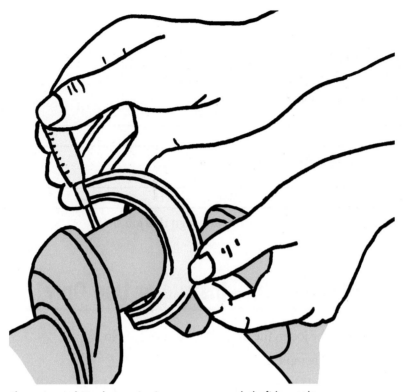

Figure 18-4. Use the proper size micrometer to measure crankshaft journals.

☐ 3. Visually check the crankshaft for the following conditions:
- Damage to the thrust bearing surfaces such as deep scratching or grooving.
  Are any defects found? Yes ___ No ___
- Deep grooves or other damage at the rear seal surface.
  Are any defects found? Yes ___ No ___
- Clogged oil passages.
  Are any defects found? Yes ___ No ___
- Loose or damaged oil gallery plugs.
  Are any defects found? Yes ___ No ___
- Stripped bolt holes.
  Are any defects found? Yes ___ No ___
- Damaged or worn keyway.
  Are any defects found? Yes ___ No ___
- Damaged reluctor ring.
  Are any defects found? Yes ___ No ___

Job Wrap-Up

☐ 1. Clean the work area and return any equipment to storage.
☐ 2. Did you encounter any problems during this procedure? Yes ___ No ___
If Yes, describe the problems:

_____

_____

What did you do to correct the problems?

_____

_____

☐ 3. Have your instructor check your work and sign this job sheet.

Performance Evaluation—Instructor Use Only

Did the student complete the job in the time allotted? Yes ___ No ___

If No, which steps were not completed? _____

How would you rate this student's overall performance on this job? _____

5–Excellent, 4–Good, 3–Satisfactory, 2–Unsatisfactory, 1–Poor

Comments: _____

_____

_____

INSTRUCTOR'S SIGNATURE_____

Project 7: Job 19—Repair Damaged Threads

After completing this job, you will be able to repair a variety of damaged threads and chase threads in a bore.

Instructions

As you read the job instructions, answer the questions and perform the tasks. Record your answers using complete sentences. Consult the proper service literature and ask your instructor for help as needed.

> ⚠ **Warning:** Before performing this job, review all pertinent safety information in the text and discuss safety procedures with your instructor.

Procedures

- [ ] 1. Obtain a piece of metal or a part with a threaded bore that has stripped threads.
- [ ] 2. Gather the tools needed to perform the following job. Refer to the tools and materials list at the beginning of the project.

Repair External Threads

> 📦 **Note:** Most stripped external threads occur on cap screws, bolts, or other parts that are usually replaced when damaged. Occasionally, the technician will be asked to repair damaged external threads. The usual reason for repairing an external thread is to remove burrs. External threads may also be repaired if hammering or cross-threading has damaged the beginning thread.

- [ ] 1. Carefully inspect the external threads and determine whether they can be repaired.
    - Are large sections of the threads missing? Yes ___ No ___
    - Have large sections of the thread been cross-threaded? Yes ___ No ___
    - Are the threads badly damaged throughout their length? Yes ___ No ___
    - Are the threads badly damaged at the spot where they will be under the most tension? Yes ___ No ___

    An answer of Yes to any of these questions usually means that the part must be replaced.

    Can the threads be repaired? Yes ___ No ___

> ⚠ **Warning** Do *not* attempt to repair badly damaged external threads, or damaged threads on critical parts. Part failure and possible injury could result.

If Yes, use one of the methods in the following three sections methods to repair the external threads.

Repair External Threads with the Die Method

- [ ] 1. Install the correct size die in the die stock.
- [ ] 2. Place the die and die stock over the external threads to be repaired.

☐ 3. Lubricate the external threads.

☐ 4. Begin turning the die stock over the threads to remove burrs or straighten a cross-threaded or damaged beginning thread.

☐ 5. After the damaged threads are repaired, remove the die and die stock by turning it in the opposite direction.

☐ 6. Thoroughly clean and reinspect the threads.

Can the part be reused? Yes ___ No ___

Repair External Threads with a Die-Type Thread Chaser

☐ 1. Install the correct size thread chaser over the external threads to be repaired. See **Figure 19-1**.

☐ 2. Lubricate the external threads.

☐ 3. Use a wrench to turn the thread chaser over the threads, **Figure 19-2**.

☐ 4. After the threads are repaired, remove the thread chaser by turning it in the opposite direction.

☐ 5. Thoroughly clean and inspect the threads.

Can the part be reused? Yes ___ No ___

Repair External Threads with a File-Type Thread Chaser

☐ 1. Lubricate the external threads.

☐ 2. Select the proper size thread chaser. Most file-type thread chasers will be four-sided, with a different thread on each side of one end, and four other thread sizes on the other end.

Figure 19-1. Install the correct thread chaser over the damaged stud. (Heli-Coil)

Figure 19-2. Turn the thread chaser with a wrench or socket to clean up the threads. This particular thread chaser can be turned in either direction. (Heli-Coil)

Project 7: Job 19 *(continued)*

☐ 3. Place the thread chaser on the damaged threads. Make sure that the high points of the chaser rest over the low points of the thread.

☐ 4. Slowly draw the thread chaser over the damaged threads, stopping frequently to inspect the work.

☐ 5. Thoroughly clean the threads and reinspect. Can the part be reused? Yes ___ No ___

Repair Internal Threads

Note: Stripped threads are usually found in aluminum assemblies, but can occur in any type of metal. Thread repair kits contain the needed drills, taps, thread repair inserts, and special mandrels for installing the inserts.

☐ 1. Determine the size and pitch of the stripped thread.

☐ 2. If necessary, place rags around the stripped thread to catch metal chips.

☐ 3. Select the proper drill bit according to the instructions of the thread repair kit.

☐ 4. Drill out the stripped threads and clean the metal chips from the hole, **Figure 19-3**.

☐ 5. Tap the hole with the appropriate tap from the thread repair kit. See **Figure 19-4**. Be sure to lubricate the tap with cutting oil before beginning the tapping operation.

☐ 6. Clean the threads to remove any remaining chips.

☐ 7. Thread the repair insert onto the correct mandrel. The insert tang should be engaged with the matching slot on the mandrel.

☐ 8. If installing the insert into an iron or steel part, lubricate it with engine oil. Do not lubricate the insert if it is to be installed in an aluminum part.

Figure 19-3. Drill out the stripped thread with the correct size drill bit. (Heli-Coil)

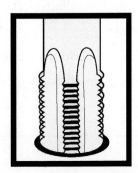

Figure 19-4. Tap the drilled hole with the proper tap. Generously lubricate the tap and hole with cutting oil. (Heli-Coil)

9. Turn the mandrel to advance it into the tapped hole, **Figure 19-5**.
10. Back the mandrel out of the hole when the insert reaches the bottom.
11. If the tang did not break off when the mandrel was removed, lightly tap it with a drift punch and hammer to remove the tang.

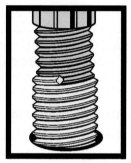

Figure 19-5. Install the thread insert with the proper tool. (Heli-Coil)

Job Wrap-Up

1. Clean and return all of the tools, and clean the work area.
2. Did you encounter any problems during this procedure? Yes ___ No ___
   If Yes, describe the problems:

   _____

   _____

   What did you do to correct the problems?

   _____

   _____

3. Have your instructor check your work and sign this job sheet.

Performance Evaluation—Instructor Use Only

Did the student complete the job in the time allotted? Yes ___ No ___

If No, which steps were not completed? _____

How would you rate this student's overall performance on this job? _____

5–Excellent, 4–Good, 3–Satisfactory, 2–Unsatisfactory, 1–Poor

Comments: _____

_____

_____

INSTRUCTOR'S SIGNATURE_____

Project 7: Job 20—Measure Cylinder Wear and Hone Cylinders

After completing this job, you will be able to measure cylinder oversize, taper, and out-of-round. You will also be able to hone cylinders.

Instructions

As you read the job instructions, answer the questions and perform the tasks. Record your answers using complete sentences. Consult the proper service literature and ask your instructor for help as needed.

Warning: Before performing this job, review all pertinent safety information in the text and discuss safety procedures with your instructor.

Procedures

Note: This job assumes that the engine block has been disassembled. Refer to Job 17 for disassembly procedures.

☐ 1. Obtain an engine to be used in this job. Your instructor may direct you to perform this job on a shop engine.

☐ 2. Identify the engine by listing the following information.

- Engine maker:

  _____

- Number of cylinders:

  _____

- Engine displacement:

  _____

☐ 3. Gather the tools needed to perform the following job. Refer to the tools and materials list at the beginning of the project.

Measure Cylinder Wear

☐ 1. Refer to the service literature to find the standard bore size.

Standard bore size:

_____

☐ 2. Obtain an inside micrometer or a telescoping gauge and an outside micrometer.

☐ 3. Take measurements at the top and bottom of the cylinder. **Figure 20-1** shows typical measurement spots.

Smallest reading:

_____

Largest reading:

_____

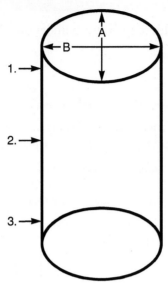

Figure 20-1. Most manufacturers call for measuring cylinders as shown. Take readings A and B about 3/8″ (10 mm) from the top and bottom, and near the center of the cylinder.

☐ 4. Check cylinder taper at the top and bottom of ring travel at right angles to the engine centerline.
Top reading:

_____

Bottom reading:

_____

☐ 5. Determine cylinder oversize by subtracting the standard bore size from the measurements made in steps 3 and 4.
Largest measured bore size reading:

_____

Standard bore size:

_____

Cylinder oversize:

_____

☐ 6. Calculate the cylinder taper by subtracting the bottom reading from the top reading.
Top of cylinder:

_____

Bottom of cylinder:

_____

Cylinder taper:

_____

Name_____

7. Take measurements at 90° apart at the top of the cylinder. Then, calculate the cylinder out-of-round by subtracting the smallest reading from the largest reading.

Largest reading:

_____

Smallest reading:

_____

Out-of-round:

_____

> **Note:** If the cylinder is more than a few thousandths oversize, tapered, or out-of round, the cylinder should be rebored to the next largest standard oversize and matching oversize rings and pistons installed. Consult your instructor if any of the measurements indicate that any of the cylinders need reboring.

8. Repeat steps 3 through 7 for all cylinders.

Hone Cylinders

> **Note:** Honing is the process used to restore the proper finish to the cylinder walls. The following task assumes that an electric drill-operated, portable hone will be used. Many shops use rigid stone hones, while others use flexible, or bead, hones. Some shops create a final finish with fine grit rigid stones or brush or plateau hone. Consult your instructor to ensure that you select the proper hone or hones for this task.

1. Clamp the hone into a low-speed electric drill.
2. Insert the hone in the first cylinder to be honed.
3. Squirt a moderate amount of hone oil onto the cylinder wall.
4. Start the drill and move it up and down the full length of the cylinder. Move the hone up and down at a rate that will produce a 50° crosshatch pattern. Note that some hone and piston ring manufacturers specify a 30° crosshatch pattern.

> **Caution:** Be careful not to pull the hone too far out of the bore or hone damage may result.

5. Turn the drill off and remove the hone. Before removing the hone, hand squeeze or adjust the stones together to prevent vertical scratches in the cylinder wall.
6. Repeat steps 2 through 5 for all cylinders.
7. Clean all cylinders with soap and hot water and rinse with clean hot water.
8. Wipe the cylinders dry with clean rags.
9. Wipe the cylinders with clean, oil-soaked rags until all of the grit is removed.

Job Wrap-Up

☐ 1. Clean the work area and return any equipment to storage.
☐ 2. Did you encounter any problems during this procedure? Yes ___ No ___
   If Yes, describe the problems:

   _____

   _____

   What did you do to correct the problems?

   _____

   _____

☐ 3. Have your instructor check your work and sign this job sheet.

Performance Evaluation—Instructor Use Only

Did the student complete the job in the time allotted? Yes ___ No ___

If No, which steps were not completed? _____

How would you rate this student's overall performance on this job? _____

5–Excellent, 4–Good, 3–Satisfactory, 2–Unsatisfactory, 1–Poor

Comments: _____

_____

_____

INSTRUCTOR'S SIGNATURE_____

Project 7:   Job 21—Inspect Connecting Rods

After completing this job, you will be able to inspect connecting rods for bending or twisting. You will also be able to check the fit of the piston (wrist) pin.

Instructions

As you read the job instructions, answer the questions and perform the tasks. Record your answers using complete sentences. Consult the proper service literature and ask your instructor for help as needed.

Warning: Before performing this job, review all pertinent safety information in the text and discuss safety procedures with your instructor.

Procedures

Note: This job assumes that the engine block has been disassembled. Refer to Job 17 for disassembly procedures.

☐   1. Obtain an engine to be used in this job. Your instructor may direct you to perform this job on a shop engine.

☐   2. Identify the engine by listing the following information.

  • Engine maker:

  _____

  • Number of cylinders:

  _____

  • Engine displacement:

  _____

☐   3. Gather the tools needed to perform the following job. Refer to the tools and materials list at the beginning of the project.

Check Piston Pin Fit

☐   1. Lightly clamp the first connecting rod and piston assembly in a vise and try to rock the piston sideways. Any movement indicates piston pin looseness, which must be corrected.

  Does the piston pin show any looseness? Yes ___ No ___

  If Yes, the piston pin looseness must be corrected. A loose pin will make a rapping noise as the engine runs. It will eventually cause the piston to break. If the piston and connecting rods have bushings, the bushings can be honed oversize and an oversize pin installed. However, on most modern vehicles, the piston and pin are replaced.

☐   2. Repeat this operation for all pistons.

Check Connecting Rods for Twisting and Bending

☐ 1. Remove the connecting rod from the first piston to be serviced. If the piston pin is held in place by snap rings, remove one snap ring and slide the pin from the piston and connecting rod. **Figure 21-1** shows the parts of a piston and rod assembly that uses snap rings to retain the piston pin. If the pin has a press fit, carefully press it from the connecting rod using the following procedure:

    a. Obtain the proper piston pin removal adapters.

    b. Ensure that the piston and connecting rods are marked for proper reassembly. **Figure 21-2** shows some places where the piston and rod can be marked for proper reassembly. Always check the service information before assembling the piston and rod.

    c. Place piston and rod in hydraulic press.

    d. Arrange adapters so that the piston will not be damaged.

    e. Carefully apply pressure to the pin to press it through the piston and rod.

    f. Closely monitor pin movement as the pin is removed. If the pin appears to bind, release the pressure and determine whether the fixtures are properly positioned.

☐ 2. Install the measuring fixture on the connecting rod. Some measuring fixtures require that the piston pin be reinserted into the connecting rod.

☐ 3. Replace the rod cap and slide the connecting rod over the measuring stand mounting rod. If necessary, adjust the mounting rod until the connecting rod fits snugly.

☐ 4 Measure the gap at several places on the measuring fixture. If you can insert a feeler gauge larger than 0.003″ (0.08 mm) between the rod and the flat plate on the measuring fixture, the rod is bent or twisted and should be replaced.

☐ 5. After checking the connecting rod, reassemble the connecting rod and piston.

☐ 6. Repeat steps 1 through 5 for all connecting rods.

Figure 21-1. Piston and connecting rod components.

Name _____

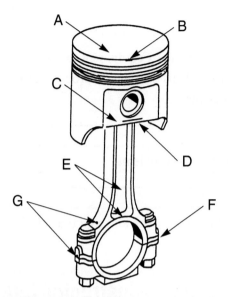

Figure 21-2. Possible locations for piston and connecting rod marks. A—On the top of the piston (may be a valve cutout area). B—Notch at the front of the piston head. C—Mark on front of piston. D—Dimple or mark on underside of piston. E—Dimple or mark on connecting rod. F—Marks or numbers on side or connecting rod and/or cap. G—Oil spurt holes.

 Note: Do *not* mix pistons, connecting rods, and pins. All parts should be replaced in the same places from which they were removed.

☐ 7. Replace the piston pin. If using a hydraulic press for a press-fit pin, select the proper adapters and use the following procedure:

    a. Make sure the marks on the piston and connecting rod are in their original position before pressing.

    b. Heavily lubricate the pin and rod bore.

    c. Begin pressing while closely monitoring pin movement.

    d. If the pin appears to bind when entering the rod, release the pressure and check adapter positions.

    e. After pressing, ensure that the pin is centered on the rod.

Job Wrap-Up

☐ 1. Clean the work area and return any equipment to storage.
☐ 2. Did you encounter any problems during this procedure? Yes ___ No ___
      If Yes, describe the problems:

      _____

      _____

      What did you do to correct the problems?

      _____

      _____

☐ 3. Have your instructor check your work and sign this job sheet.

Performance Evaluation—Instructor Use Only

Did the student complete the job in the time allotted? Yes ___ No ___

If No, which steps were not completed? _____

How would you rate this student's overall performance on this job? _____

5–Excellent, 4–Good, 3–Satisfactory, 2–Unsatisfactory, 1–Poor

Comments: _____

_____

_____

INSTRUCTOR'S SIGNATURE_____

Project 7: Job 22—Inspect Pistons and Replace Piston Rings

After completing this job, you will be able to inspect pistons for excessive wear and replace piston rings.

Instructions

As you read the job instructions, answer the questions and perform the tasks. Record your answers using complete sentences. Consult the proper service literature and ask your instructor for help as needed.

> ⚠️ **Warning:** Before performing this job, review all pertinent safety information in the text and discuss safety procedures with your instructor.

Procedures

> **Note:** This job assumes that the engine block has been disassembled. Refer to Job 17 for disassembly procedures.

☐ 1. Obtain an engine to be used in this job. Your instructor may direct you to perform this job on a shop engine.

☐ 2. Identify the engine by listing the following information.

- Engine maker:

_____

- Number of cylinders:

_____

- Engine displacement:

_____

☐ 3. Gather the tools needed to perform the following job. Refer to the tools and materials list at the beginning of the project.

Visually Inspect Pistons

☐ 1. If necessary, clean the piston thoroughly.

☐ 2. Visually inspect the pistons for severe scuffing on the skirts and ring land areas, cracks at the piston pin bosses, erosion or indentations on the piston head, and other obvious damage.

Is there any obvious damage? Yes ___ No ___

If Yes, explain:

_____

> **Note:** A diagonal (sideways) wear pattern extending from the top to the bottom of the piston skirt indicates a bent or twisted connecting rod. Refer to Job 21 for information on checking connecting rod condition.

Measure Piston Clearance

☐ 1. Measure the diameter of the piston across the skirts.
   Piston diameter:
   _____

☐ 2. Find the cylinder diameter, the measurement taken at the bottom of the cylinder. Refer to Job 20 as needed.
   Cylinder diameter:
   _____

☐ 3. Subtract the piston diameter from the cylinder diameter to determine piston clearance.
   Cylinder diameter:
   _____

   Piston diameter:
   _____

   Piston clearance:
   _____

☐ 4. Repeat steps 1 through 3 for all other cylinders and pistons.

> **Caution:** If the piston clearance is excessive, do not install the piston, as it will be noisy and wear the cylinder and rings. The piston can be knurled to increase the skirt diameter, or a larger-diameter piston can be substituted.

Remove Piston Rings and Clean Ring Grooves

☐ 1. Place the piston and rod assembly in a vise with the piston skirt resting on top of the vise jaws so it cannot swivel. Clamp the vise jaws around the connecting rod.

☐ 2. Use a ring expander to remove the piston rings from the piston, **Figure 22-1**. Open the rings only enough to clear the piston lands.

☐ 3. Remove carbon from the inside of the ring grooves with a ring groove cleaner. Select the correct-width scraper for each groove and be careful not to remove any metal.

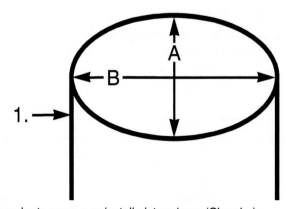

Figure 22-1. Use a ring expander to remove or install piston rings. (Chrysler)

Name _____

> **Note:** If a groove cleaner is not available, a broken piston ring can be used to clean the ring grooves.

☐ 4. Repeat steps 1 through 3 for all other pistons.

Check Ring Groove Wear

☐ 1. Measure the ring side clearance as demonstrated in **Figure 22-2**. Fit a ring into the top and middle ring grooves. Determine the largest size feeler gauge that will fit between the side of each groove and ring. The gauge size is the ring side clearance for that ring. The top piston groove will usually be the most worn.

Specified side clearance for the top ring:

_____

Specified side clearance for the middle ring:

_____

Measured side clearance of the top ring:

_____

Measured side clearance of the middle ring:

_____

☐ 2. Repeat this operation for all other pistons. Replace any pistons that have excessive ring groove wear.

Check Piston-to-Bore Clearance

> **Note:** The piston-to-bore clearance of a cylinder and piston must be measured using the same piston that will be installed in the cylinder during reassembly. Measuring piston-to-bore clearance using a different piston will result in an inaccurate reading.

☐ 1. Select the piston that will be installed in the cylinder during reassembly.
☐ 2. Remove the piston rings if not already removed.
☐ 3. Install a spring scale on the piston.

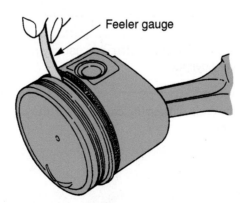

Feeler gauge

Figure 22-2. Use a feeler gauge to check piston ring-to-groove clearance. (Chrysler)

4. Place the piston in the cylinder bore with the piston skirts in the same relative position that they would have with the piston installed.

5. Insert a feeler gauge between the piston skirt and bore. Special narrow feeler gauges are available for this procedure.

6. Pull the piston out of the cylinder using the spring scale.

7. Record the spring scale reading:

   Reading: _____

   Specified reading: _____

8. Change feeler gauges until the proper spring gauge reading is obtained.

   If the gauge reading is too high, substitute a thinner feeler gauge and repeat steps 4 through 7.

   If the gauge reading is too low, substitute a thicker feeler gauge and repeat steps 4 through 7.

   When the correct spring gauge reading is obtained, the feeler gauge size used at the time is the piston-to-bore clearance.

   Note: If piston-to-bore clearance is excessive, consult your instructor. Excessive piston-to-bore clearance must be corrected to avoid piston slap and resulting piston and cylinder wear. Possible corrections include knurling the piston skirts or boring the block oversize and installing oversize pistons.

Check Ring Gap

1. Place a compression ring squarely into the cylinder. Push it to the bottom of ring travel with the head of the piston.

2. Determine the largest size feeler gauge that will fit in the gap between the ends of the ring. This is the ring gap.

   Specified upper compression ring gap:

   _____

   Specified lower compression ring gap:

   _____

   Measured upper compression ring gap:

   _____

   Measured lower compression ring gap:

   _____

   Note: If all cylinders are the same size, it is usually not necessary to check the ring gap on every cylinder.

3. If the ring gap is too small, the ends of the ring can be carefully filed to increase the gap. If the gap is too large, replace the ring.

Install Piston Rings

☐ 1. Install the oil rings on the piston.
☐ 2. Check the ring markings to ensure that they are installed facing up.
☐ 3. Install the lower compression ring by hand or with a ring expander.
☐ 4. Install the top compression ring by hand or with a ring expander.
☐ 5. Stagger the ring gaps so that they do not line up. See **Figure 22-3**.
☐ 6. Repeat this operation for all other pistons.

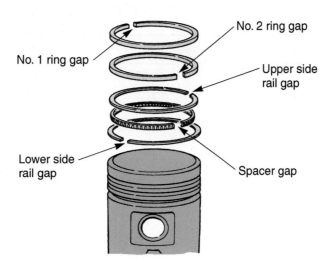

No. 2 ring gap
No. 1 ring gap
Upper side rail gap
Lower side rail gap
Spacer gap

Figure 22-3. Install the piston rings so the gaps are staggered. (Chrysler)

Job Wrap-Up

☐ 1. Clean the work area and return any equipment to storage.
☐ 2. Did you encounter any problems during this procedure? Yes ___ No ___
   If Yes, describe the problems:

   _____

   _____

   What did you do to correct the problems?

   _____

   _____

☐ 3. Have your instructor check your work and sign this job sheet.

Performance Evaluation—Instructor Use Only

Did the student complete the job in the time allotted? Yes ____ No ____

If No, which steps were not completed? _____

How would you rate this student's overall performance on this job? _____

5–Excellent, 4–Good, 3–Satisfactory, 2–Unsatisfactory, 1–Poor

Comments: _____

_____

_____

INSTRUCTOR'S SIGNATURE_____

Project 7: Job 23—Inspect Balance Shafts, the Vibration Damper, and the Oil Pump

After completing this job, you will be able to inspect balance shafts, vibration dampers, and oil pumps.

Instructions

As you read the job instructions, answer the questions and perform the tasks. Record your answers using complete sentences. Consult the proper service literature and ask your instructor for help as needed.

> **Warning:** Before performing this job, review all pertinent safety information in the text and discuss safety procedures with your instructor.

Procedures

> **Note:** This job assumes that the engine block has been disassembled. Refer to Job 17 for disassembly procedures.

☐ 1. Obtain an engine to be used in this job. Your instructor may direct you to perform this job on a shop engine.

☐ 2. Identify the engine by listing the following information.
- Engine maker:

_____

- Number of cylinders:

_____

- Engine displacement:

_____

☐ 3. Gather the tools needed to perform the following job. Refer to the tools and materials list at the beginning of the project.

Inspect Balance Shafts

☐ 1. Check the condition of the balance shaft journals and any bearings.
Condition observed
Pitting ___ Scratches ___ Ridges ___ Overheating ___ Damaged keyway ___ Other (describe):

_____

_____

☐ 2. Measure the balance shaft journals with a micrometer.
Bearing journal #1
Specified diameter: _____   Measured diameter: _____
Bearing journal #2
Specified diameter: _____   Measured diameter: _____

Bearing journal #3

Specified diameter: _____   Measured diameter: _____

Bearing journal #4

Specified diameter: _____   Measured diameter: _____

☐ 3. If the balance shaft is damaged or excessively worn, replace it.

Check the Vibration Damper

☐ 1. Visually check the vibration damper (sometimes called a harmonic balancer) for the following:

   • Missing or extruded (pushed out) rubber between the damper sections, **Figure 23-1**.

   • A damaged keyway.

   Are any defects found? Yes ___ No ___

☐ 2. Place the vibration damper on a flat surface and look for misalignment between the damper sections.
   Is any misalignment found? Yes ___ No ___

☐ 3. If the vibration damper has any obvious problems, such as a separated rubber insert or misalignment, replace it.

Inspect the Oil Pump

☐ 1. Check the oil pump for obvious problems such as a damaged or loose pick-up tube or torn or clogged intake screen.
   Were any obvious problems found? Yes ___ No ___
   If Yes, describe the problems:

   _____

   _____

Figure 23-1. Check for damage to the rubber insert between the hub and outer weight. This damper has light nicks on the rubber, but is otherwise OK.

Name _____

Figure 23-2. Check for obvious signs of pump scoring or other wear. A—Pump plate. B—Pump gears. C—Circumference of pump outer gear.

☐ 2. Disassemble the oil pump, if it is not already disassembled.

☐ 3. Check the pump for obvious wear and scoring, **Figure 23-2**.

☐ 4. Using feeler gauges, check clearances between the pump gears and the pump cover and pump body. Maximum allowable clearance:

_____

Actual reading:

_____

Is the actual reading within specifications? Yes ___ No ___

☐ 5. Check the pressure control valves:

    a. Carefully move the pressure regulator valve against spring tension with a small screwdriver. If the valve snaps back with spring pressure, it is free in its bore.

    b. Ensure that the pressure relief valve or check ball moves freely by moving it with a small screwdriver. If the relief valve or check ball moves, it is usually good.

    c. Inspect the regulator valve bore and relief valve seat for wear or damage.

    d. Replace any defective pressure control valve parts.

6. If the oil pump has damaged, scored, or excessively worn parts, replace it.

> **Note:** Some oil pump gears and endplates can be replaced without replacing the pump housing, but this should only be done when the other oil pump parts are in **excellent** condition.

Job Wrap-Up

1. Clean the work area and return any equipment to storage.
2. Did you encounter any problems during this procedure? Yes ___ No ___
   If Yes, describe the problems:

   _____

   _____

   What did you do to correct the problems?

   _____

   _____

3. Have your instructor check your work and sign this job sheet.

Performance Evaluation—Instructor Use Only

Did the student complete the job in the time allotted? Yes ___ No ___

If No, which steps were not completed? _____

How would you rate this student's overall performance on this job? _____

5–Excellent, 4–Good, 3–Satisfactory, 2–Unsatisfactory, 1–Poor

Comments: _____

_____

_____

INSTRUCTOR'S SIGNATURE_____

Project 8

Servicing the Cylinder Head(s) and Valve Train

Introduction

As a technician, you will likely be required to perform cylinder head service, usually called a "valve job." Cylinder heads can be made of cast iron, aluminum, or magnesium with two, three, or four valves per cylinder. A variety of camshaft placements and valve train designs can be used to open and close the valves. All engines have at least one camshaft and most engines have valve lifters.

When the camshaft is located in the block, pushrods are used. This arrangement is known as *cam-in-block engine*. When the cylinder head contains the camshaft, the arrangement is known as an *overhead camshaft* (or simply *overhead cam*) *engine*. Some overhead camshaft engines have hydraulic lash adjusters that take up the valve train clearance. The service procedures described in this project apply generally to all cylinder heads and will provide you with a guideline for complete engine top-end and front-end service.

In Job 24, you will disassemble and inspect a cylinder head. In Job 25, with the cylinder head disassembled, you will inspect valve train components for wear and damage by observation and by the use of measuring tools. In Job 26, you will learn how to resurface (grind) valves and valve seats. You will reassemble the cylinder head in Job 27. In Job 28, you will inspect camshaft drives and other valve timing components. You will adjust the engine's valves in Job 29. In Job 30, you will learn how to replace a valve seal without removing the cylinder head, thereby saving time and expense.

Project 8 Jobs

- Job 24—Disassemble and Inspect a Cylinder Head
- Job 25—Inspect and Service Valve Train Parts
- Job 26—Resurface and Inspect Valves and Valve Seats
- Job 27—Assemble a Cylinder Head
- Job 28—Inspect Valve Timing Components
- Job 29—Adjust Valves
- Job 30—Replace Valve Seals with the Cylinder Head Installed

Tools and Materials

The following list contains the tools and materials that may be needed to complete the jobs in this project. The items used will depend on the make and model of the vehicle being serviced.

- Vehicle in need of valve seal replacement.
- Cylinder head to be serviced.
- Service information.
- Valve spring compressor.
- Air pressure adapter that can be installed in a spark plug opening.
- Air pressure hose.
- Brass hammer.
- Straightedge.
- Feeler gauges.
- Inside micrometers.
- Outside micrometers.
- Telescoping gauges.
- Valve grinding machine.
- Valve seat grinder or cutter set.
- Air or electric drill.
- Rotary wire brush.
- Hand tools.
- Air-powered tools.
- Safety glasses and other protective equipment.

Safety Notice

Before performing these jobs, review all pertinent safety information in the text and review safety information with your instructor.

Name_____

Date_____ Class _____

After completing this job, you will be able to inspect, disassemble, and clean a cylinder head.

Instructions

As you read the job instructions, answer the questions and perform the tasks. Record your answers using complete sentences. Consult the proper service literature and ask your instructor for help as needed.

> ⚠ **Warning:** Before performing this job, review all pertinent safety information in the text and discuss safety procedures with your instructor.

Procedures

☐ 1. Obtain a cylinder head assembly to be used in this job.

☐ 2. Gather the tools needed to perform the following job. Refer to the tools and materials list at the beginning of the project.

Inspect the Cylinder Head

☐ 1. Place the head on a bench or suitable head repair fixture.

☐ 2. Identify the cylinder head by listing the following information.

- Engine maker:

_____

- Number of cylinders:

_____

- Engine displacement:

_____

☐ 3. Visually inspect the head for damage. **Figure 24-1** shows an obviously burned valve.

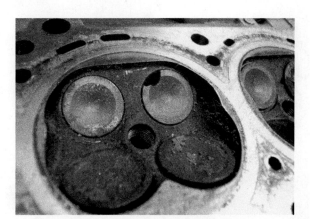

Figure 24-1. The exhaust valve in this photograph is obviously burned. Sometimes a burned valve is harder to identify, especially if it has just started to fail.

Describe any damage found:

_____

_____

☐ 4. Place a straightedge across the surface of the head at various angles and attempt to slide different size feeler gauge blades between the straightedge and the head. This checks the cylinder head for a warped sealing surface. See **Figure 24-2**. Acceptable warpage is around 0.003″ (0.08 mm) over any 6″ (150 mm) surface.

What is the largest blade that will fit between the straightedge and head?

_____

If the head is warped more than the specification, what should be done next?

_____

_____

Remove the Camshaft(s)

> **Note:** This section applies only to cylinder heads with overhead camshafts.

☐ 1. If the rocker arm shafts have not yet been removed, make sure they are marked so they can be reinstalled in the proper locations. Then, remove the rocker arm shaft and the followers.

☐ 2. Remove the camshaft timing advance mechanism if used.

☐ 3. Remove the rocker arm assemblies if not removed earlier. On some vehicles, the rocker arm bolts also hold the bearing caps in place.

☐ 4. Remove the bolts holding the camshaft bearing caps to the head.

☐ 5. Remove the caps from the head, **Figure 24-3**.

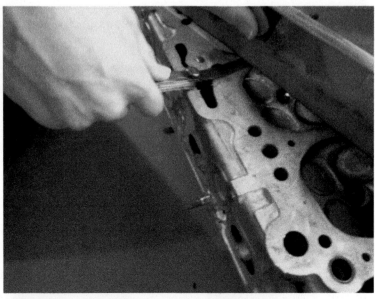

Figure 24-2. Use a feeler gauge and straightedge to check the head for warpage.

Project 8: Job 24 *(continued)*

Figure 24-3. Once the fasteners are removed, the camshaft bearing cap can be lifted from the head.

- [ ] 6. Mark the caps and place them in order for reassembly.
- [ ] 7. Remove the camshaft from the head.

Remove the Valves

- [ ] 1. Strike the valve spring retainers to loosen them. Use a brass hammer to avoid damaging the valve stems.
- [ ] 2. Place a valve spring compressor over the first valve to be removed.
- [ ] 3. Depress the spring compressor and remove the valve spring keepers.
- [ ] 4. Open the spring compressor and remove the retainer and spring. Do *not* remove the valves and valves seals at this time.
- [ ] 5. Place the parts together in a container or on a clean area of the bench.
- [ ] 6. Repeat steps 2 through 5 for the other valves in the head. Place the parts in order so they can be reinstalled in the same position.

Inspect the Cylinder Head Parts

- [ ] 1. Pull each valve partially out of the head and wiggle it in the valve guide, **Figure 24-4**. Measure the movement with a dial indicator for maximum accuracy. If the valve moves more than 1/32″ (0.8 mm), the guide is worn excessively. List the guide wear measurements in the spaces provided:

Valve 1: _____   Valve 2: _____

Valve 3: _____   Valve 4: _____

Valve 5: _____   Valve 6: _____

Valve 7: _____   Valve 8: _____

Valve 9: _____   Valve 10: _____

Valve 11: _____   Valve 12: _____

Valve 13: _____   Valve 14: _____

Valve 15: _____   Valve 16: _____

Figure 24-4. If the valve moves too much, the guide, and possibly the valve stem, is worn excessively.

Note: Worn valve guides must be repaired or replaced to avoid excessive oil consumption, valve noise, and valve and seat damage. If any valves are excessively worn, consult your instructor before proceeding. Some manufacturers require that the internal diameter of the guides be checked with a small inside micrometer or telescoping gauge.

☐ 2. Check the condition of the valve springs.
   - Visually inspect each valve spring for squareness and obvious damage.
   - Use a small ruler to measure valve spring free height.

   Are any problems found? Yes ___ No ___
   If Yes, describe:

   _____
   _____

Note: Some springs have tighter (more closely spaced) coils on one end. This is normal.

☐ 3. Visually inspect the valve retainers and locks for damage or excessive wear. Look for wear that would cause the retainer to come loose during engine operation.

   Are any defective parts found? Yes ___ No ___
   If Yes, describe:

   _____
   _____

Name _____

☐ 4. Visually inspect the valve retainer grooves in the valve stem. Grooves should show no wear or damage.

Are any retainer grooves defective? Yes ___ No ___

If Yes, describe:

_____

_____

Note: Any parts found to be defective in steps 2, 3, and 4 should be replaced.

☐ 5. Remove the valve stem seals if they are not already removed.

☐ 6. Remove the valves, one at a time, keeping them in order.

Caution: If the valve does not slide easily from the head, the stem may have widened where it contacts the rocker arm. This is called "mushrooming." A mushroomed valve stem must be filed down to allow it to slide through the valve guide. Do not hammer a mushroomed valve out of the head.

☐ 7. Inspect each valve for wear or damage by comparing it to the valves shown in **Figure 24-5**.

Are any valves too badly worn or damaged to reuse? Yes ___ No ___

Explain your answer:

_____

_____

_____

_____

☐ 8. Scrape all gasket material from the head sealing surface and use a wire wheel and drill to remove carbon from the combustion chamber. Thoroughly wash the head after removing all debris.

Warning: Wear eye protection while using a wire brush.

☐ 9. Check the cylinder head for obvious cracks.

Are any cracks present? Yes ___ No ___

If Yes, what should you do next?

_____

_____

_____

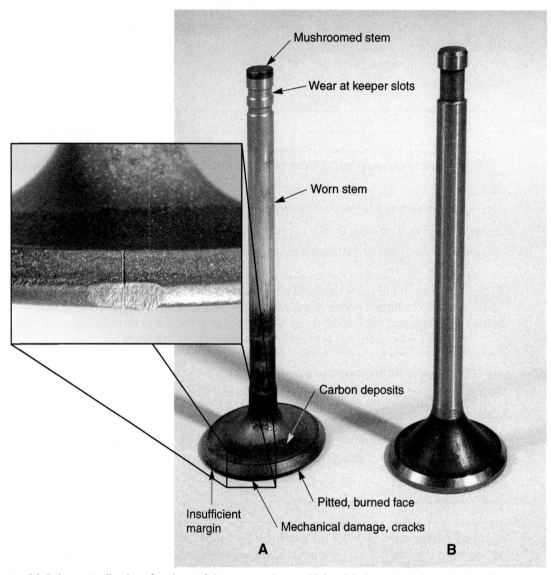

Figure 24-5. Inspect all valves for signs of damage and wear. Valve A is burned and cracked and has mechanical damage. Note the common areas of wear and the close-up of the damage on valve A. Valve B is in good used condition.

 Note: If you suspect that the head has a crack that cannot be found by visual inspection, it will be necessary to check the head by magnetic or black light methods. Ask your instructor if further crack testing should be preformed. Magnetic crack detection will not work on aluminum cylinder heads.

10. If the head has an overhead camshaft or camshafts, check the camshaft journal caps and head for scoring or metal transfer. See **Figure 24-6**. Replace any damaged parts.

Project 8: Job 24 *(continued)*

Figure 24-6. Check the condition of the cap and head where the camshaft bearings ride.

 Note: A few overhead camshaft heads will have separate camshaft bearing inserts. These inserts should be replaced as part of head service.

☐ 11. Check the camshaft for wear as outlined in Job 25.

Job Wrap-Up

☐ 1. Clean the work area and return any equipment to storage.

☐ 2. Did you encounter any problems during this procedure? Yes ___ No ___
If Yes, describe the problems:

_____

_____

What did you do to correct the problems?

_____

_____

☐ 3. Have your instructor check your work and sign this job sheet.

Performance Evaluation—Instructor Use Only

Did the student complete the job in the time allotted? Yes ___ No ___

If No, which steps were not completed? _____

How would you rate this student's overall performance on this job?_____

5–Excellent, 4–Good, 3–Satisfactory, 2–Unsatisfactory, 1–Poor

Comments: _____

_____

_____

INSTRUCTOR'S SIGNATURE_____

Name _____

Date _____ Class _____

After completing this job, you will be able to check valve train components for wear and damage.

Instructions

As you read the job instructions, answer the questions and perform the tasks. Record your answers using complete sentences. Consult the proper service literature and ask your instructor for help as needed.

> ⚠️ **Warning:** Before performing this job, review all pertinent safety information in the text and discuss safety procedures with your instructor.

Procedures

☐ 1. Obtain an engine or cylinder head assembly to be used in this job.

☐ 2. Gather the tools needed to perform the following job. Refer to the tools and materials list at the beginning of the project.

☐ 3. Identify the valve train parts and the type of valve train being serviced.

Describe the valve train being serviced, including the location of the cam, the type of lifters or lash adjusters, and the number of valves per cylinder:

_____

_____

_____

> **Note:** Valve lifters can be divided into two general types—mechanical and hydraulic. Use the procedure that applies to the lifter being checked. A hydraulic lifter has oil holes and a plunger that allow its overall length to vary with hydraulic pressure.

Inspect Hydraulic Lifters

☐ 1. Examine the lower part of the lifter where it contacts the camshaft, **Figure 25-1**.
   Do you find any wear? Yes ___ No ___

☐ 2. Check for flat spots on the roller (for roller lifters), **Figure 25-2**.
   Do you find any flat spots? Yes ___ No ___

☐ 3. Check for a loose roller pin.
   Is the pin loose? Yes ___ No ___

☐ 4. Examine the push rod contact surface.
   Is any wear visible? Yes ___ No ___

☐ 5. Check for wear or damage to the clip holding the internal parts to the body.
   Is any wear or damage noted? Yes ___ No ___

☐ 6. Inspect the oil passages for sludge deposits.
   Is sludge noted? Yes ___ No ___

Figure 25-1. Check the lifter body for damage to the camshaft contact surface, wear and scoring where the body contacts the engine block, and sludge buildup in the oil holes. The camshaft contact surface of this hydraulic lifter is badly pitted.

Figure 25-2. Roller lifters should be checked for flat spots on the rollers. If a roller has a flat spot, the camshaft lobe is probably damaged. This roller lifter appears to be in good condition.

- [ ] 7. If instructed to do, check the leakdown rate of the valve lifters.

   What are the results of the leakdown test?

   _____

   _____

- [ ] 8. Replace any lifters that are excessively worn.

Inspect Mechanical Lifters

- [ ] 1. Examine the lower part of the lifter where it contacts the camshaft.

   Do you find any wear? Yes ___ No ___

- [ ] 2. Check for flat spots on the roller (for roller lifters).

   Do you find any flat spots? Yes ___ No ___

- [ ] 3. Check for a loose roller pin.

   Is the pin loose? Yes ___ No ___

- [ ] 4. Check the push rod contact surface.

   Is wear evident? Yes ___ No ___

- [ ] 5. Replace any lifters that are excessively worn.

Project 8: Job 25 (continued)

Inspect Valve Lash Adjusters

 Note: Lash adjusters are installed in the head and control the clearance of the drive train parts in an overhead cam engine. **Figure 25-3** shows the common types of hydraulic lash adjusters and compares them to a lifter in a push rod–type valve train.

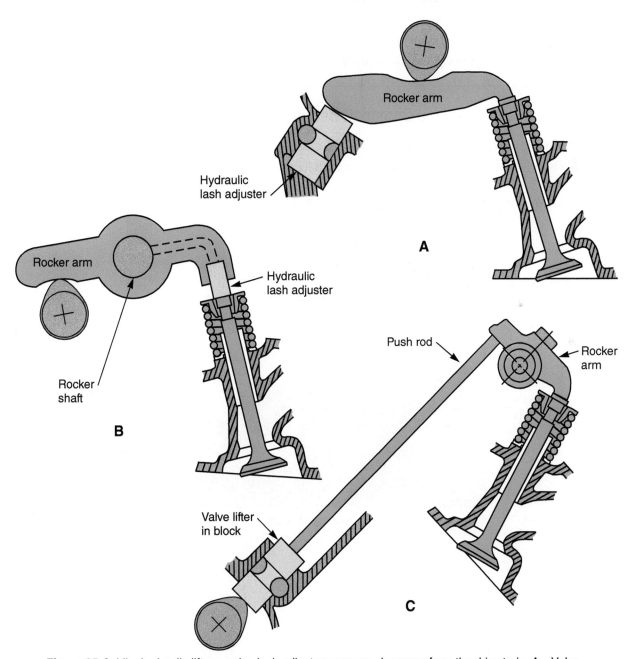

Figure 25-3. Like hydraulic lifters, valve lash adjusters remove clearance from the drive train. A—Valve lash adjusters may be placed opposite of the valve. B—Valve lash adjusters may be part of the rocker arm. C—Compare the placement and function of the lash adjusters in A and B to the lifter shown here.

☐ 1. Check for wear at the point where the lash adjuster contacts the other moving parts of the drive train and where it contacts the cylinder head.

Is any wear noted? Yes ___ No ___

☐ 2. Check for wear or damage to the clip, pin, or snap ring holding the internal parts in the lash adjuster body.

Is any wear or damage noted? Yes ___ No ___

☐ 3. Inspect the oil passages for sludge deposits.

Is any sludge noted? Yes ___ No ___

☐ 4. Check lash adjuster leakdown, if possible and if instructed to do so.

Describe the results of the leakdown test:

_____

Inspect the Camshaft(s) and Camshaft Bearings

☐ 1. Remove the camshaft from the engine, if necessary.

☐ 2. Visually check the condition of the camshaft lobes. **Figure 25-4** shows a camshaft with badly worn lobes.

Are the lobes on the camshaft worn? Yes ___ No ___

Figure 25-4. The lobes on this camshaft are excessively worn.

Project 8: Job 25 *(continued)*

☐ 3. Check lobe lift using a micrometer. **Figure 25-5** shows a typical procedure. Record the results of the micrometer tests in the following chart.

Specification:	Reading:
Specification:	Reading:
Specification:	Reading:
Specification:	Reading:
Specification:	Reading:
Specification:	Reading:
Specification:	Reading:
Specification:	Reading:
Specification:	Reading:
Specification:	Reading:
Specification:	Reading:
Specification:	Reading:
Specification:	Reading:
Specification:	Reading:
Specification:	Reading:
Specification:	Reading:

☐ 4. Check the camshaft bearing journal size with a micrometer. See **Figure 25-5**. Record the results of the micrometer tests in the following chart.

Specification:	Reading:
Specification:	Reading:
Specification:	Reading:
Specification:	Reading:
Specification:	Reading:
Specification:	Reading:

☐ 5. Check camshaft straightness using V-blocks. The camshaft should turn between the blocks with no noticeable wobble. For extreme accuracy, a dial indicator can be used.

6. If the camshaft is equipped with a reluctor ring, examine it for damage. Was any damage found? Yes ___ No ___

☐ 7. Check the bearing surfaces for wear and scoring, **Figure 25-6**.

Is wear or scoring present? Yes ___ No ___

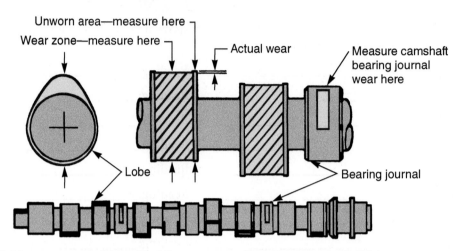

Figure 25-5. Measure camshaft lobe lift at the wear zone. To determine camshaft lobe wear, measure the camshaft lobe at the unworn area and subtract the measurement taken at the wear zone. (Chrysler)

Figure 25-6. A visual inspection of the camshaft bearing surfaces will reveal many problems. Note that this cylinder head does not have separate bearing inserts. This is true of most overhead cam engines.

8. Inspect each bearing to ensure that it is properly aligned with its bore.

Were any bearings misaligned? Yes ___ No ___

If Yes, which one(s): _____

Note: If the camshaft bearings are installed in the engine block, you can use an inside micrometer or a telescoping gauge to measure the inside diameters of the bearings to check for wear and out-of-round. The bearing clearance on some overhead camshafts can be checked with Plastigage. Consult with your instructor to determine if you should perform these checks.

Name _____

☐ 9. Check the thrust surfaces for wear and scoring.

Is wear or scoring present? Yes ___ No ___

 Note: If the camshaft is worn or bent, it must be replaced. Worn or damaged bearing inserts can be replaced without replacing the block or head. If a cylinder head does not have bearing inserts, the head must be replaced if the bearing surfaces are damaged.

Inspect Rocker Arms and Rocker Arm Shafts

☐ 1. Visually check the rocker arms. Refer to **Figure 25-7**. Check each rocker arm for the following conditions:

- Wear at the points where the rocker arm contacts other moving parts.

- Wear where the rocker arm oscillates on the rocker shaft.

- Clogged oil passages in the rocker arm.

- Bending, cracking, or other damage to the rocker arm.

Is any damage present? Yes ___ No ___

If Yes, describe the damage:

_____

_____

_____

Note: Damaged rocker arms and related parts should be replaced. If the camshaft directly moves the rocker arm, it should also be replaced. If the rocker arm is worn where is contacts the rocker arm shaft, **Figure 25-8**, the shaft should also be replaced.

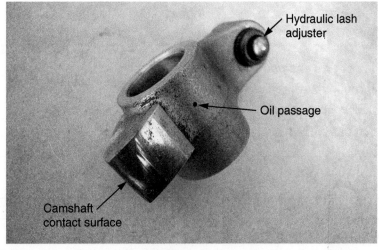

Figure 25-7. Check the rocker arm for sludge buildup and for wear at the points where it contacts other parts.

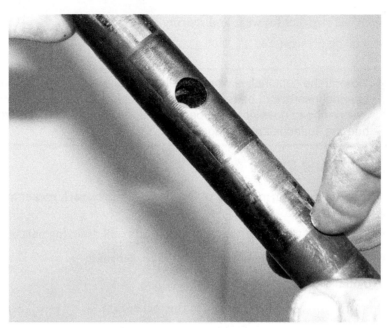

Figure 25-8. Check the rocker arm shaft for wear. If your fingernail hangs up solidly in the rocker arm groove, the shaft should be replaced.

Inspect Push Rods

☐   1. Visually check the push rods for wear and bending. If the push rods are hollow, check the interior for sludge buildup.

☐   2. Roll each push rod on a flat surface to check for bends.

      Are any of the push rods bent? Yes ____ No ____

☐   3. Replace any bent or otherwise damaged push rod.

> **Note:** It is usually easier to replace badly clogged push rods rather than attempt to clean them.

Job Wrap-Up

☐   1. Clean the work area and return any equipment to storage.

☐   2. Did you encounter any problems during this procedure? Yes ____ No ____

      If Yes, describe the problems:

      _____

      _____

      What did you do to correct the problems?

      _____

      _____

☐   3. Have your instructor check your work and sign this job sheet.

Name_____

Performance Evaluation—Instructor Use Only

Did the student complete the job in the time allotted? Yes ___ No ___

If No, which steps were not completed? _____

How would you rate this student's overall performance on this job?_____

5–Excellent, 4–Good, 3–Satisfactory, 2–Unsatisfactory, 1–Poor

Comments: _____

_____

_____

INSTRUCTOR'S SIGNATURE_____

Notes

Project 8: Job 26—Resurface and Inspect Valves and Valve Seats

After completing this job, you will be able to resurface valves and valve seats.

Instructions

As you read the job instructions, answer the questions and perform the tasks. Record your answers using complete sentences. Consult the proper service literature and ask your instructor for help as needed.

> ⚠ **Warning:** Before performing this job, review all pertinent safety information in the text and discuss safety procedures with your instructor.

Procedures

☐ 1. Obtain a disassembled cylinder head assembly to be used in this job.

☐ 2. Gather the tools needed to perform the following job. Refer to the tools and materials list at the beginning of the project.

Resurface (Grind) Valves

> **Note:** Obtain your instructor's permission before using the valve grinding machine.

☐ 1. Prepare the valve grinding machine by checking condition of the grinding wheel, the cooling fluid level, and all related hardware. Be sure you are familiar with all machine controls.

☐ 2. Determine the valve face angle and set the valve grinding machine to produce this angle. Most modern vehicles have either a 45° or 30° angle, but this should be confirmed by checking the manufacturer's service literature.

☐ 3. Adjust the grinder to the appropriate angle by loosening the chuck hold-down nut and swiveling the chuck mechanism until its degree marks line up. Some makers call for a 1° interference angle. In these cases, you would set the chuck to cut an angle 1° less than the desired angle. For example, for a 45° valve, you would adjust the valve grinding machine so it produces a 44° cut.

☐ 4. Insert the valve into the valve grinder. Check that the chuck jaws grasp the valve stem on the machined portion of the stem nearest the valve head.

☐ 5. Turn the grinder on and ensure that the valve is not wobbling in the chuck. If the valve wobbles, remount it and recheck.

> **Note:** If the wobble cannot be corrected, the valve is bent and must be replaced.

☐ 6. Make sure cooling fluid is flowing over the valve head. The valve should be positioned so the valve face is parallel with the cutting surface of the stone. Turn the depth wheel a little at a time to move the stone toward the valve so parallelism can be checked and adjusted.

☐ 7. Slowly advance the stone toward the valve. As soon as the stone touches the valve, begin moving the valve back and forth across the grinding surface of the stone.

Warning: Wear safety glasses or a face shield when using a valve grinder.

☐ 8. Watch the face of the valve carefully as you move it across the surface of the grinding stone. As soon as the valve face has been refinished, back off the depth wheel.

☐ 9. Turn off the grinder and check the valve margin, **Figure 26-1**. If the margin is less than 1/32″ (0.8 mm), the valve should be replaced. A thin valve margin will cause the valve to burn.

How wide is the valve margin?

_____

Caution: The minimum margin varies by manufacturer. Check the appropriate service information before proceeding.

☐ 10. Dress the end of the valve stem by mounting the valve in the V-block on the opposite end of the grinder chuck. Remove as little metal as possible, generally less than 0.010″ (0.25 mm).

How much material was removed from the valve stem?

_____

☐ 11. Repeat steps 4 through 10 for all valves.

Resurface (Grind) Valve Seats

Caution: Some valve seats are actually hardened inserts. They should be replaced instead of ground.

☐ 1. Determine and locate the correct size of stone or cutter. The cutter should be the proper angle and slightly larger than the head of the valve.

Cutter angle:

_____

Cutter size:

_____

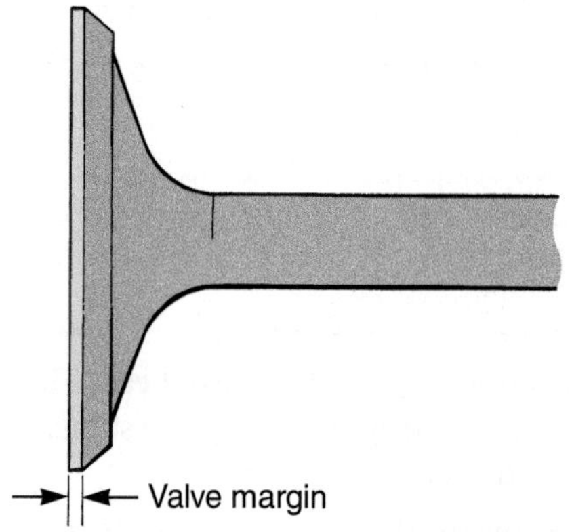

← Valve margin

Figure 26-1. The valve margin must meet the minimum specification after the valve is refaced. (Chrysler)

Name _____

Note: Valve seat angles may vary by manufacturers. Consult the appropriate service information to select the proper cutters.

☐ 2. Clean the valve guide and install the cutter assembly.
☐ 3. Carefully check the fit of the stone or cutter to confirm that it is the correct one.
☐ 4. Lubricate the cutter assembly then begin the cutting process. Remove only enough metal to eliminate pitting and ridges on the seat.
☐ 5. Inspect the valve seat to ensure that it has been sufficiently cleaned up.
☐ 6. Use deep and shallow angle cutters or stones to narrow the valve seat as necessary. **Figure 26-2** shows typical seat angles.
☐ 7. Repeat steps 2 through 6 for all valve seats.

Check the Valve Face-to-Seat Contact

☐ 1. Make a series of pencil marks on the valve seat face.

Note: This procedure can also be performed using a special valve checking compound, often referred to as Prussian blue.

☐ 2. Place the valve in the cylinder head.
☐ 3. Press the valve down onto the seat and turn it about one-fourth of a revolution.
☐ 4. Remove the valve and inspect the pencil marks on the valve seat face. Spots where the pencil marks are rubbed off indicate the contact point between the valve face and the seat. The contact point should be in the middle of the valve face. It should be about 1/16″ (1.5 mm) wide and extend all of the way around the face.

Are the pencil marks wiped off all of the way around the valve face? Yes ___ No ___
Explain:

_____
_____

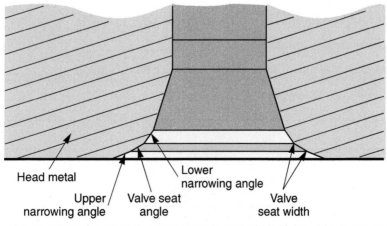

Figure 26-2. The valve seat must be cut to the proper angle and width. If the width is too small, the valve may burn; too wide, and the valve may stick.

☐ 5. Repeat steps 1 through 4 for all valve seats.
☐ 6. Measure the valve stem height:

   a. Obtain valve height specifications.

   b. Place the valve in its proper position in the cylinder head.

   c. Press the valve into the seat.

   d. Using a special measuring tool or small ruler, measure the valve stem height from the spring seat on the head.

   e. If the valve stem height is too low, replace the valve. If the height is too high, remove a small amount of metal from the valve stem tip until the correct height is reached.

> **Caution:** The valve stem tip is hardened for only a small distance. If the valve tip requires excessive metal removal, replace the valve.

Job Wrap-Up

☐ 1. Clean the work area and return any equipment to storage.
☐ 2. Did you encounter any problems during this procedure? Yes ___ No ___
   If Yes, describe the problems:

   _____

   _____

   What did you do to correct the problems?

   _____

   _____

☐ 3. Have your instructor check your work and sign this job sheet.

Performance Evaluation—Instructor Use Only

Did the student complete the job in the time allotted? Yes ___ No ___

If No, which steps were not completed? _____

How would you rate this student's overall performance on this job?_____

5–Excellent, 4–Good, 3–Satisfactory, 2–Unsatisfactory, 1–Poor

Comments: _____

_____

_____

INSTRUCTOR'S SIGNATURE_____

Project 8:   Job 27—Assemble a Cylinder Head

After completing this job, you will be able to properly assemble a cylinder head.

Instructions

As you read the job instructions, answer the questions and perform the tasks. Record your answers using complete sentences. Consult the proper service literature and ask your instructor for help as needed.

> **Warning:** Before performing this job, review all pertinent safety information in the text and discuss safety procedures with your instructor.

Procedures

- [ ] 1. Obtain a disassembled cylinder head assembly to be used in this job.
- [ ] 2. Gather the tools needed to perform the following job. Refer to the tools and materials list at the beginning of the project.

Install the Valves

- [ ] 1. Oil the valve stem and install the valve in its original position.
- [ ] 2. Use a valve stem height gauge to check the stem height. If the valve stem height is correct, proceed to the next step. If the step height is incorrect, ask your instructor what steps to take next.

> **Note:** Checking valve stem height is especially important if the valve faces or seats have been resurfaced.

- [ ] 3. If the valve stem uses an umbrella seal, install the seal now, **Figure 27-1**.
- [ ] 4. Assemble the valve spring(s) and retainer over the valve stem.
- [ ] 5. Use the valve spring compressor to compress the spring.
- [ ] 6. If the valve stem uses an O-ring seal, install the seal now. See **Figure 27-2**.
- [ ] 7. Install the valve keepers, **Figure 27-3**. Keepers can be held in place with heavy grease.
- [ ] 8. Release the spring compressor and ensure that all parts are in their proper place.
- [ ] 9. Check the valve spring assembled height with a small ruler, as in **Figure 27-4**. If the assembled height is correct, proceed to the next step. If the assembled height is not correct, ask your instructor what steps should be taken next.
- [ ] 10. Repeat steps 1 through 9 for all valves.

Figure 27-1. Carefully slide the umbrella seal over the valve stem. (Fel-Pro)

Figure 27-2. Place the O-ring in the proper groove on the valve. (Fel-Pro)

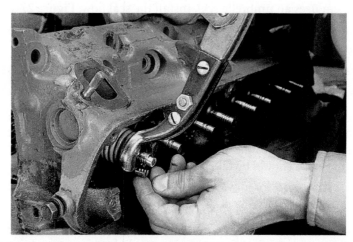

Figure 27-3. Be sure that the valve retainers are in place before releasing the spring. (Fel-Pro)

Name_____

Figure 27-4. Check the valve spring assembled height using a small ruler.

Install the Camshaft(s)

 Note: This section applies only to cylinder heads with overhead camshafts. If the engine you are working on uses an in-block camshaft, skip this section.

☐ 1. Lubricate the cam journals.
☐ 2. Install the cam bearings if used.
☐ 3. Place the camshaft into position.
☐ 4. Place the bearing caps into position. Be sure to line up any oil holes, **Figure 27-5.**
☐ 5. If desired, check bearing clearance with Plastigage. This may require temporarily performing step 6.

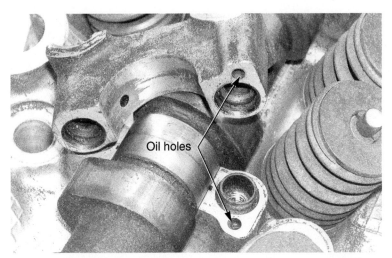

Figure 27-5. Oil holes in the bearing cap and head must line up. If oil does not reach the moving parts of the valve train, they will be ruined almost immediately.

☐ 6. Install the rocker arm shafts if they are part of the bearing cap assembly. Tighten the fasteners one-half turn at a time, starting with the middle bolts. Remember that the compressed valve springs will be pushing against the rocker shaft.

☐ 7. Torque the cap bolts to specifications.

☐ 8. If the camshaft has a timing advance mechanism, install it now.

Job Wrap-Up

☐ 1. Clean the work area and return any equipment to storage.

☐ 2. Did you encounter any problems during this procedure? Yes ___ No ___
If Yes, describe the problems:

_____

_____

What did you do to correct the problems?

_____

_____

☐ 3. Have your instructor check your work and sign this job sheet.

Performance Evaluation—Instructor Use Only

Did the student complete the job in the time allotted? Yes ___ No ___

If No, which steps were not completed? _____

How would you rate this student's overall performance on this job?_____

5–Excellent, 4–Good, 3–Satisfactory, 2–Unsatisfactory, 1–Poor

Comments: _____

_____

_____

INSTRUCTOR'S SIGNATURE_____

Name _____

Date _____ Class _____

After completing this job, you will be able to inspect valve timing components and set valve timing.

Instructions

As you read the job instructions, answer the questions and perform the tasks. Record your answers using complete sentences. Consult the proper service literature and ask your instructor for help as needed.

> ⚠️ **Warning:** Before performing this job, review all pertinent safety information in the text and discuss safety procedures with your instructor.

Procedures

☐ 1. Obtain a vehicle to be used in this job. Your instructor may direct you to perform this job on a shop vehicle or engine.

☐ 2. Gather the tools needed to perform the following job. Refer to the tools and materials list at the beginning of the project.

Check the Operation of a Variable Valve Timing Mechanism

> 🔧 **Caution:** Perform the following test only if it is specifically mentioned in the manufacturer's service literature. Do *not* ground any computer control system wire without checking the service literature.

☐ 1. Locate the solenoid that controls the flow of oil to the variable valve timing mechanism. The solenoid may be installed on the valve cover, on the side of the engine, or in the head under the valve cover.

☐ 2. Determine which solenoid wire receives a ground signal from the ECM by consulting the appropriate wiring diagram.

☐ 3. Start the engine and raise the engine speed to about 2500 rpm.

☐ 4. Ground the solenoid signal wire and observe engine operation. There should be a noticeable change in engine speed and sound as the valve timing changes.

Does the engine speed change? Yes ___ No ___

Does the sound of the engine change? Yes ___ No ___

If the engine speed or sound does not change, the solenoid is defective, the internal advance mechanism is stuck or leaking, or the engine's oil pressure is low. Make further checks according to the manufacturer's service information.

Check Camshaft Drive Parts

Note: Placement of sprockets and belts or chains varies greatly by design. Some overhead camshaft engines may have as many as four camshaft sprockets.

- [ ] 1. Remove the camshaft drive parts from the engine as necessary.
- [ ] 2. Visually inspect the condition of gears and drive sprockets. See **Figure 28-1**.
- [ ] 3. Check the condition of the timing chain or belt. Most checks can be made visually. A worn chain will have excessive slack. A worn belt will have cracks and possible missing teeth.
- [ ] 4. Check the condition of the chain or belt tensioner.
  - a. Check the tensioner for obvious physical damage.
  - b. When possible, check the tensioner spring pressure with the proper special tool.

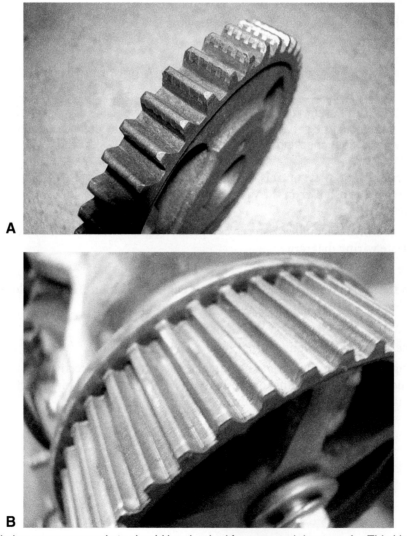

Figure 28-1. Timing gears or sprockets should be checked for wear and damage. A—This kind of wear on a timing gear indicates that the gear should be replaced. B—This sprocket is in good condition.

Project 8: Job 28 *(continued)*

    c. Check hydraulic tensioners for leaks, lack of oil, or other damage.

> **Note:** Refer to Job 32 for procedures for replacing camshaft drive parts. Drive parts should be replaced as a set.

Check Variable Valve Timing Components

☐   1. Inspect the variable valve timing mechanism for the following:
        Leakage: Yes ____ No ____
        Cracks: Yes ____ No ____
        Damaged mounting hardware: Yes ____ No ____

Job Wrap-Up

☐   1. Clean the work area and return any equipment to storage.

☐   2. Did you encounter any problems during this procedure? Yes ____ No ____
        If Yes, describe the problems:

        _____

        _____

        What did you do to correct the problems?

        _____

        _____

☐   3. Have your instructor check your work and sign this job sheet.

Performance Evaluation—Instructor Use Only

Did the student complete the job in the time allotted? Yes ____ No ____

If No, which steps were not completed? _____

How would you rate this student's overall performance on this job?_____

5–Excellent, 4–Good, 3–Satisfactory, 2–Unsatisfactory, 1–Poor

Comments: _____

_____

_____

INSTRUCTOR'S SIGNATURE_____

Notes

Project 8: Job 29—Adjust Valves

After completing this job, you will be able to adjust mechanical and hydraulic valves.

Instructions

As you read the job instructions, answer the questions and perform the tasks. Record your answers using complete sentences. Consult the proper service literature and ask your instructor for help as needed.

> ⚠ **Warning:** Before performing this job, review all pertinent safety information in the text and discuss safety procedures with your instructor.

Procedures

☐ 1. Obtain a vehicle to be used in this job. Your instructor may direct you to perform this job on a shop vehicle or engine.

☐ 2. Gather the tools needed to perform the following job. Refer to the tools and materials list at the beginning of the project.

☐ 3. Remove the engine valve cover(s) to reveal the valve adjustment device.

> **Note:** On some overhead camshaft engines, clearance is adjusted by changing lifters or adding shims at the lifters. Consult the manufacturer's service information for these procedures.

☐ 4. Determine whether the engine uses mechanical or hydraulic valve lifters.

Mechanical: ___ Hydraulic: ___

> **Note:** The following sections provide instructions for adjusting valves with mechanical lifters and adjusting valves with hydraulic lifters. Use the procedure that is appropriate for the type of lifters used in your vehicle. Skip the procedure that does not apply.

Adjust Valves—Mechanical Valve Lifters

☐ 1. Obtain the proper specification for valve clearance.

Specification for intake valve: _____ inches or millimeters (circle one).

Does the specification call for the engine to be warmed up? Yes ___ No ___

Specification for exhaust valve:_____ inches or millimeters (circle one).

Does the specification call for the engine to be warmed up? Yes ___ No ___

☐ 2. By hand, turn the crankshaft until the camshaft lobe for the valve to be adjusted points away from the lifter.

☐ 3. Loosen the adjuster locknut.

☐ 4. Insert the proper thickness feeler gauge between the valve and the rocker arm. See **Figure 29-1**.

☐ 5. Turn the adjuster while moving the feeler gauge between the valve and rocker arm. When there is a light drag on the feeler gauge, clearance is correct.

☐ 6. Tighten the adjuster locknut while holding the adjuster in position.

☐ 7. Recheck the adjustment to ensure that the adjuster did not move when the locknut was tightened.

☐ 8. Repeat steps 2 through 7 for the other valves.

☐ 9. Start the engine and recheck the adjustment by inserting a feeler gauge between the valve and rocker arm.

Does the feeler gauge fit between the valve and rocker arm? Yes ___ No ___

Are any valves noisy (clattering or tapping sounds)? Yes ___ No ___

Does the noise stop when the feeler gauge is inserted between the valve and rocker arm? Yes ___ No ___

Adjust Valves—Hydraulic Valve Lifters

☐ 1. Place shielding around the valve assemblies to reduce oil spray.

☐ 2. Start the engine.

☐ 3. Loosen the valve adjuster locknut on the first valve to be adjusted. Note that not all rocker assemblies are equipped with valve adjuster locknuts.

☐ 4. Back off the valve adjuster until the valve begins to make a clattering noise. See **Figure 29-2**.

☐ 5. Tighten the adjuster until the noise just stops.

☐ 6. Tighten the adjuster an additional number of turns as specified by the service literature. If the rocker assembly is equipped with a valve adjuster locknut, retighten it. Be careful not to allow the valve adjuster to rotate.

☐ 7. Repeat steps 3 through 6 for all other engine valves.

☐ 8. Remove all splash shields from the valve assemblies.

☐ 9. Replace the valve cover(s) using a new gasket as needed.

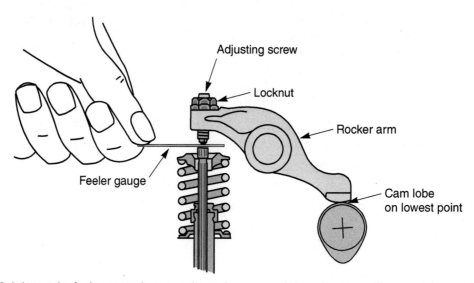

Figure 29-1. Insert the feeler gauge between the rocker arm and the valve stem. The cam lobe must be at its lowest point (putting no pressure on the valve train).

Name_____

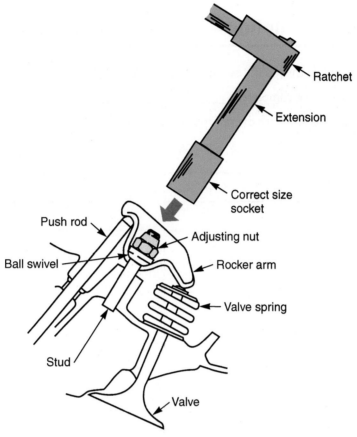

Figure 29-2. Adjust the valve until it just stops clattering, then turn the adjuster in an additional specified number of turns. The adjusting nut shown here has an interference fit and does not use a locknut.

Job Wrap-Up

☐ 1. Clean the work area and return any equipment to storage.
☐ 2. Did you encounter any problems during this procedure? Yes ___ No ___
      If Yes, describe the problems:

      _____

      _____

      What did you do to correct the problems?

      _____

      _____

☐ 3. Have your instructor check your work and sign this job sheet.

Performance Evaluation—Instructor Use Only

Did the student complete the job in the time allotted? Yes ___ No ___

If No, which steps were not completed? _____

How would you rate this student's overall performance on this job?_____

5–Excellent, 4–Good, 3–Satisfactory, 2–Unsatisfactory, 1–Poor

Comments: _____

_____

_____

INSTRUCTOR'S SIGNATURE_____

Project 8:   Job 30—Replace Valve Seals with the Cylinder Head Installed

After completing this job, you will be able to replace valve seals without remove the cylinder head from the vehicle.

Instructions

As you read the job instructions, answer the questions and perform the tasks. Record your answers using complete sentences. Consult the proper service literature and ask your instructor for help as needed.

> ⚠️ **Warning:** Before performing this job, review all pertinent safety information in the text and discuss safety procedures with your instructor.

Procedures

☐   1. Obtain a vehicle to be used in this job. Your instructor may direct you to perform this job on a shop vehicle or engine.

☐   2. Gather the tools needed to perform the following job. Refer to the tools and materials list at the beginning of the project.

☐   3. Remove the valve cover over the valve needing the seal replacement.

Record the number of the cylinder requiring valve seal replacement: _____.

☐   4. Remove the rocker arm from the valve requiring seal replacement.

Is the seal on an exhaust valve or an intake valve?

_____

> **Note:** All valves in this cylinder must be closed or the procedure will not work. Bring the piston to the top of its compression stroke or back off all other valve rocker arms on this cylinder.

☐   5. Remove the spark plug from the cylinder with the valve seal that needs replacement.

☐   6. Install an air pressure adapter in the plug opening.

☐   7. Introduce air pressure into cylinder. This will hold the valve up as the spring is compressed.

☐   8. Install a special spring compressor tool on the cylinder head. **Figure 30-1** shows a valve spring compressor used on an overhead camshaft engine.

☐   9. Compress the valve spring with the valve spring compressor.

☐   10. Remove the valve spring keepers.

☐   11. Release the pressure on the spring and remove the spring and retainer from the head.

☐   12. Remove the valve seal.

Which type of seal is used?

- Umbrella seal: ____

- Positive seal: ____

- O-ring seal: ____

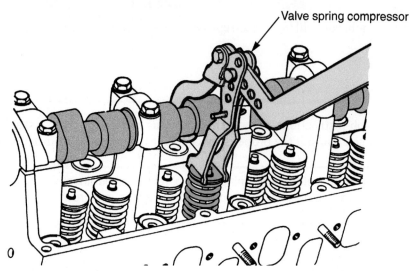

Figure 30-1. This valve spring compressor hooks around the camshaft to allow compression of the spring and removal of the valve. (Chrysler)

13. If the seal is an umbrella or positive seal type, install the replacement seal over the valve stem. Use a seal protector to prevent seal damage. See **Figure 30-2**.

14. Place the spring and retainer over the valve stem.

15. Compress the valve spring with the valve spring compressor.

16. If the seal is an O-ring type, lubricate the seal and place it in its groove on the valve stem. See **Figure 30-3**.

 Caution: Be sure that the O-ring is installed in the seal groove, not the keeper groove.

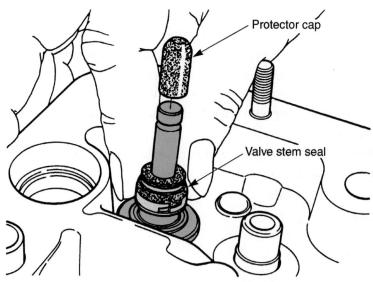

Figure 30-2. Umbrella and positive seals are installed between the valve stem and cylinder head. (Chrysler)

Name_____

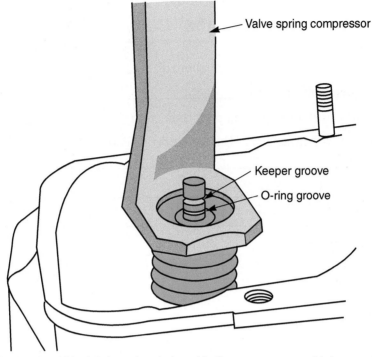

Figure 30-3. The O-ring should be lubricated and placed in the proper groove. Make sure that the O-ring is not twisted.

☐ 17. Install the spring keepers.
☐ 18. Release pressure on the spring and allow the spring to rise to its normal position.
☐ 19. Check that the keepers are properly in place.
☐ 20. Release the air pressure from the cylinder.
☐ 21. Remove the air pressure adapter from the spark plug opening.
☐ 22. Reinstall the spark plug.
☐ 23. Reinstall the rocker arm and valve cover. Use a new valve cover gasket as necessary.

Job Wrap-Up

☐ 1. Clean the work area and return any equipment to storage.
☐ 2. Did you encounter any problems during this procedure? Yes ___ No ___
   If Yes, describe the problems:

   _____

   _____

   What did you do to correct the problems?

   _____

   _____

☐ 3. Have your instructor check your work and sign this job sheet.

Performance Evaluation—Instructor Use Only

Did the student complete the job in the time allotted? Yes ___ No ___

If No, which steps were not completed? _____

How would you rate this student's overall performance on this job?_____

5–Excellent, 4–Good, 3–Satisfactory, 2–Unsatisfactory, 1–Poor

Comments: _____

_____

_____

INSTRUCTOR'S SIGNATURE_____

Project 9

Reassembling and Reinstalling an Engine

Introduction

Although there are many types of engines, the general steps for disassembly and reassembly are similar for all types. The most important parts of the job are to make sure that parts are installed in order, thereby preventing unnecessary removal and reinstallation, and to make sure that all fasteners are tightened to the proper torque values. In Job 31, you will install the crankshaft, piston assemblies, and other bottom end components to create a properly assembled short block. In Job 32, you will assemble the engine to the long block stage by adding the heads, valve train components, and valve timing components to the short block. In Job 33, you will complete the engine reassembly. You will reinstall the engine into the vehicle in Job 34.

Project 9 Jobs

- Job 31—Reassemble the Engine's Bottom End
- Job 32—Install the Cylinder Head(s) and Valve Train
- Job 33—Complete the Engine Reassembly
- Job 34—Reinstall the Engine

Tools and Materials

The following list contains the tools and materials that may be needed to complete the jobs in this project. The items used will depend on the make and model of the vehicle being serviced.

- Engine to be reassembled.
- Applicable service information.
- Ring compressor.
- Torque wrench.
- Engine lift.
- Engine lifting hook and chain assembly.
- Engine holding fixture.
- Dial indicator.
- Engine oil.
- Hand tools.
- Air-powered tools.
- Safety glasses and other protective equipment.

Safety Notice

Before performing these jobs, review all pertinent safety information in the text and review safety information with your instructor.

Project 9: Job 31—Reassemble the Engine's Bottom End

After completing this job, you will be able to reassemble an engine to the short block stage.

Instructions

As you read the job instructions, answer the questions and perform the tasks. Record your answers using complete sentences. Consult the proper service literature and ask your instructor for help as needed.

⚠️ **Warning:** Before performing this job, review all pertinent safety information in the text and discuss safety procedures with your instructor.

Procedures

☐ 1. Obtain an unassembled engine to be used in this job. Your instructor may direct you to perform this job on a shop engine.
   * Make of engine:

   _____

   * Number of cylinders:

   _____

   * Cylinder arrangement (V-type, inline, etc.):

   _____

   * Cooling system: Liquid ____ Air ____

☐ 2. Gather the tools needed to perform the following tasks. Refer to the tools and materials list at the beginning of the project.

☐ 3. Before starting assembly of the engine, look up the following torque specifications in the service manual. Record the information in the appropriate spaces.
   Oil pump fasteners: _____ ft-lb _____ N·m
   Main bearing cap fasteners: _____ ft-lb _____ N·m
   Connecting rod cap fasteners: _____ ft-lb _____ N·m

Install a Two-Piece Rear Main Oil Seal

Note: If a one-piece oil seal is used, skip this section and refer to the *Install a One-Piece Rear Main Oil* section of this job. One-piece seals are installed after the crankshaft and bearing caps.

☐ 1. Lubricate the sealing lip of the new seal with clean engine oil or assembly lube.

☐ 2. Install one-half of the seal into the main bearing cap so that the sealing lip will face the inside of the block when the cap is installed.

☐ 3. Install the other half of the seal into block, again making sure that the sealing lip faces the inside of the block.

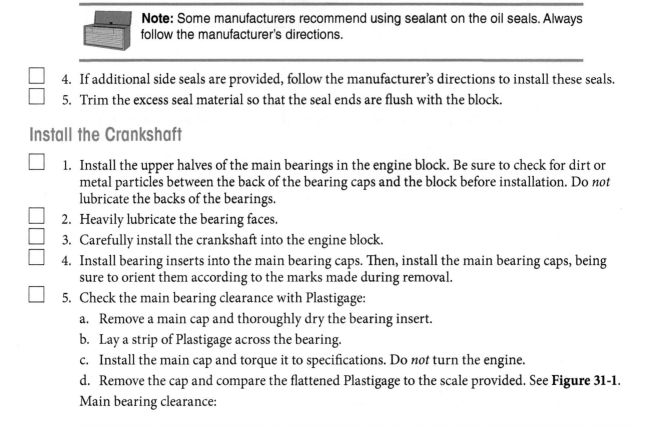

Note: Some manufacturers recommend using sealant on the oil seals. Always follow the manufacturer's directions.

☐ 4. If additional side seals are provided, follow the manufacturer's directions to install these seals.

☐ 5. Trim the excess seal material so that the seal ends are flush with the block.

Install the Crankshaft

☐ 1. Install the upper halves of the main bearings in the engine block. Be sure to check for dirt or metal particles between the back of the bearing caps and the block before installation. Do *not* lubricate the backs of the bearings.

☐ 2. Heavily lubricate the bearing faces.

☐ 3. Carefully install the crankshaft into the engine block.

☐ 4. Install bearing inserts into the main bearing caps. Then, install the main bearing caps, being sure to orient them according to the marks made during removal.

☐ 5. Check the main bearing clearance with Plastigage:

    a. Remove a main cap and thoroughly dry the bearing insert.

    b. Lay a strip of Plastigage across the bearing.

    c. Install the main cap and torque it to specifications. Do *not* turn the engine.

    d. Remove the cap and compare the flattened Plastigage to the scale provided. See **Figure 31-1**.

    Main bearing clearance:

_____

Is the main bearing clearance acceptable? Yes ___ No ___

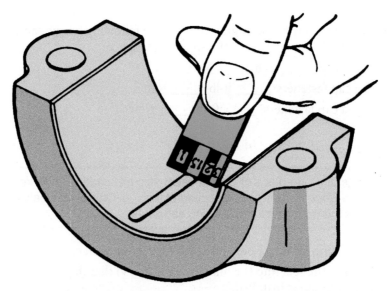

Figure 31-1. The width of the flattened Plastigage indicates the bearing clearance. (Chrysler)

Project 9: Job 31 *(continued)*

If No, select the correct oversize or undersize main bearings:

a. Add or subtract the Plastigage reading from the specified clearance.
Result:

_____

b. Select the correct oversize or undersize bearing to bring the clearance to the proper specification.

c. Replace the original bearing with the replacement bearing and recheck clearance with Plastigage.

☐ 6. Remove the Plastigage. Install and tighten the main bearing cap fasteners to the proper torque.

☐ 7. Ensure that the crankshaft turns easily with the main bearing caps properly torqued.

☐ 8. Check crankshaft endplay using a dial indicator:

a. Install the dial indicator on one end of the crankshaft. The dial indicator plunger should be parallel with the crankshaft centerline. **Figure 31-2** shows a typical dial indicator setup.

b. Push the crankshaft forward.

c. Zero the dial indicator.

d. Push the crankshaft backward.

e. Note the dial indicator reading:

_____

Is the reading within specifications? Yes ___ No ___

If No, an oversize or undersize thrust bearing must be installed, as described in the next step.

Note: Some manufacturers call for checking endplay with a feeler gauge between the crankshaft and the thrust bearing.

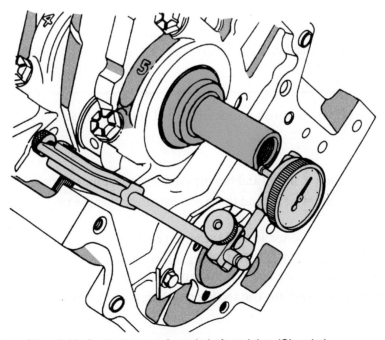

Figure 31-2. A setup of the dial indicator to record crankshaft endplay. (Chrysler)

9. If necessary, install an oversize or undersize thrust bearing:
   a. Add or subtract the dial indicator reading from the specified endplay.
      Result:

   _____

   b. Select the correct oversize or undersize bearing to bring the endplay to the proper specification.
   c. Replace the original bearing with the replacement bearing and recheck the endplay.

> **Note:** Some engines have a separate thrust bearing, while on others the thrust bearing is attached to one of the main bearings.

Install a One-Piece Rear Main Oil Seal

> **Note:** Skip this section if a two-piece oil seal was installed with the crankshaft.

1. Lubricate the inside of the new seal with assembly lube.

> **Note:** Some manufacturers recommend applying sealant to the outside of the seal. Always follow the manufacturer's directions.

2. Carefully line up the new seal with the matching grooves in the block and main bearing cap. Make sure the sealing lip of the seal faces the inside of block.
3. Carefully drive the seal into position using the proper seal driver. Use only light hammer blows and be careful not to damage the seal.

> **Note:** Installation of some seals may require the use of a special seal driver.

4. Inspect the seal to make sure it is properly seated and undamaged.

Install the Pistons

1. Decide which piston to install and heavily oil the piston, pin, and rings.
2. Place the ring compressor around the piston, ensuring that the ring compressor is facing the proper direction.
3. Tighten the ring compressor around the piston rings.
4. Remove the rod cap and install the bearing insert in the rod. Oil the exposed surface of the bearing. Install the bearing insert in the cap, but do not oil it at this time.
5. Place protective caps over the connecting rod studs of the piston.

Project 9: Job 31 *(continued)*

☐ 6. Install the piston by placing the piston and rod assembly into the cylinder and gently tapping the piston into the cylinder with a hammer handle, **Figure 31-3**. Be sure that the rod studs slip over the crankshaft journal without marring it.

☐ 7. Place the connecting rod cap over the rod studs, being sure that it faces in the proper direction.

☐ 8. Check the rod bearing clearance with Plastigage:

    a. Remove the connecting rod cap and thoroughly dry the bearing insert.

    b. Lay a strip of Plastigage across the bearing.

    c. Install and torque the rod cap to specifications. Do *not* turn the engine.

    d. Remove the cap and compare the flattened Plastigage to the scale provided.

Rod bearing clearance:

_____

Is the rod bearing clearance acceptable? Yes ___ No ___

If Yes, go to step 9.

If No, oversize or undersize bearings must be installed:

    a. Add or subtract the Plastigage reading from the desired clearance.
      Result:

_____

    b. Select the correct bearing inserts to bring the clearance to the proper specification.

    c. Replace the original rod and cap inserts with the replacement inserts and recheck the clearance with Plastigage.

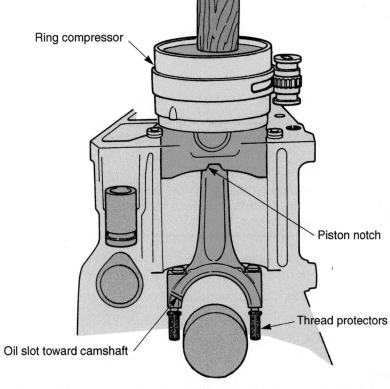

Figure 31-3. Carefully install the piston so there is no damage to the rings or crankshaft journals. (Chrysler)

☐ 9. Remove the Plastigage. Oil the exposed surface of the rod cap bearing insert. Place the connecting rod cap over the rod studs, being sure that it faces in the proper direction.

☐ 10. Install and tighten the rod nuts to the proper torque.

Torque:

_____

☐ 11. Install long bolts in two of the bores in the crankshaft's flywheel flange. Place a large screwdriver between the bolts and use it as a lever to turn the crankshaft.

Does the crankshaft turn easily? Yes ___ No ___

If No, remove the piston and rod assembly, identify and correct the problem, and reinstall the assembly.

☐ 12. Repeat steps 1 through 11 for all piston and rod assemblies.

Install the Balance Shafts

☐ 1. Install the balance shaft drive chain if used.

☐ 2. Lubricate the balance shaft bearings as necessary.

☐ 3. Place the balance shaft in position on the engine.

☐ 4. Install the balance shaft drive chain on the balance shaft.

Caution: Be sure to line up all balance shaft, crankshaft, and chain timing marks. If this is not done, the engine will vibrate severely.

☐ 5. Install all bearing or housing fasteners and tighten them to the proper torque.

Install the Oil Pump and Oil Pan

☐ 1. Rotate the engine block until the bottom of the engine faces up.

☐ 2. Place the oil pump in position on the engine block and install and tighten the oil pump bolts.

Note: Some oil pumps are driven by a shaft from the distributor or distributor adapter gear. If the pump shaft can only be installed from the bottom, install it as part of the oil pump assembly.

Other oil pumps are installed in the engine front cover and driven directly by the crankshaft. Refer to the manufacturer's service literature for information on how to assemble and install these types of pumps.

☐ 3. If your instructor instructs you to do so, pre-lubricate the bearings by following the directions provided by the manufacturer of the pre-lubrication equipment.

☐ 4. Scrape the oil pan and block mating surfaces to remove old gasket material.

☐ 5. Place the oil pan gaskets and seals on the engine block. Use the proper type of sealer, if required.

☐ 6. Place the oil pan on the block.

☐ 7. Install and tighten the oil pan fasteners. Use the correct sequence and tighten the fasteners to the proper torque.

Name _____

Install In-Block Camshafts

Note: This procedure is used only if the camshaft is installed in the block. This procedure assumes that the camshaft bearings have been inspected and/or replaced.

☐ 1. Lubricate the camshaft bearings and camshaft journals.
☐ 2. Slowly insert the camshaft into the block, making sure that the cam lobes do not damage the cam bearings.
☐ 3. When the camshaft is fully installed, ensure that it turns freely in the block.
☐ 4. Install the thrust plate or other device that holds the cam in the block.
☐ 5. Install the block's rear camshaft plug, if necessary.
☐ 6. Check camshaft endplay:

    a. Install a dial indicator on the camshaft at the thrust plate.

    b. Pull the camshaft forward.

    c. Zero the dial indicator.

    d. Push the camshaft rearward.

    e. Read and record the endplay.

    Endplay: _____

Is the endplay within specifications? Yes ____ No ____

If No, consult your instructor for the steps needed to correct the endplay.

Note: On many engines, the camshaft gear must be temporarily installed to take endplay readings.

Job Wrap-Up

☐ 1. Clean and return all of the tools and clean the work area.
☐ 2. Did you encounter any problems during this procedure? Yes ____ No ____

    If Yes, describe the problems:

_____

_____

    What did you do to correct the problems?

_____

_____

☐ 3. Have your instructor check your work and sign this job sheet.

Performance Evaluation—Instructor Use Only

Did the student complete the job in the time allotted? Yes ___ No ___

If No, which steps were not completed? _____

How would you rate this student's overall performance on this job? _____

5–Excellent, 4–Good, 3–Satisfactory, 2–Unsatisfactory, 1–Poor

Comments: _____

_____

_____

INSTRUCTOR'S SIGNATURE_____

Name_____

Date_____ Class _____

After completing this job, you will be able to install the cylinder heads and valve train components on a short block.

Instructions

As you read the job instructions, answer the questions and perform the tasks. Record your answers using complete sentences. Consult the proper service literature and ask your instructor for help as needed.

> ⚠ **Warning:** Before performing this job, review all pertinent safety information in the text and discuss safety procedures with your instructor.

Procedures

> **Note:** This job assumes that the crankshaft, pistons, balance shafts, oil pump, and oil pan have been installed on the block. Refer to Job 31 for procedures for installing these components.

☐ 1. Obtain an engine to be used in this job. Your instructor may direct you to perform this job on a shop engine.

- Make of engine:

   _____

- Number of cylinders:

   _____

- Cylinder arrangement (V-type, inline, etc.):

   _____

- Cooling system: Liquid ____ Air ____

☐ 2. Gather the tools needed to perform the following tasks. Refer to the tools and materials list at the beginning of the project.

☐ 3. Before starting assembly of the engine, look up the following torque specifications in the service manual. Record the information in the appropriate spaces.
Cylinder head fasteners: _____ ft-lb _____ N•m
Intake manifold/plenum fasteners: _____ ft-lb _____ N•m
Rocker arm fasteners (if applicable): _____ ft-lb _____ N•m
Valve cover fasteners: _____ ft-lb _____ N•m
Timing mechanism fasteners: _____ ft-lb _____ N•m
Front cover fasteners: _____ ft-lb _____ N•m

Install the Cylinder Head(s)

☐ 1. Rotate the engine until the top of the engine faces up.

☐ 2. Scrape the block and head mating surfaces clean. Remove all traces of old gasket material from the engine. The mating surfaces should be perfectly clean, as shown in **Figure 32-1**.

☐ 3. Place the head gasket on the block. Gasket direction is usually stamped on the gasket material. Use gasket sealer only if recommended by the engine manufacturer.

☐ 4. Carefully position the cylinder head on the block. Aligning pins help in installation and reduce the chance of damaging the head gasket.

☐ 5. Squirt a small amount of oil on the head bolt threads and thread them into the block by hand. Use a speed handle or ratchet (*not* an impact wrench) to turn them until they seat in the block. Do not tighten the bolts at this time.

> **Note:** Many modern engines use a torque plus angle (torque-to-yield) tightening method. The bolts are torqued to a relatively low value, then tightened by turning the bolt an additional fraction of a turn, such as 1/4 turn (an angle of 90°). If the engine must be reassembled using this method, consult the manufacturer's service literature for the proper torque values and angle.

☐ 6. Using a torque wrench, tighten the head bolts to one-half of their full torque specification. Follow the tightening order or sequence given in the service literature. Draw the tightening sequence in **Figure 32-2**. If there is no sequence, begin at the center and alternate sides, tightening outward.

What is one-half of the head bolt torque specification?

_____

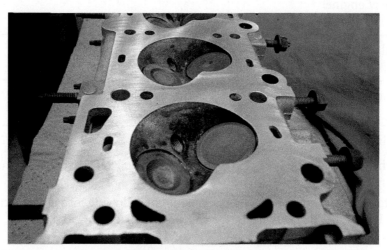

Figure 32-1. The block and head mating surfaces should be perfectly clean and straight.

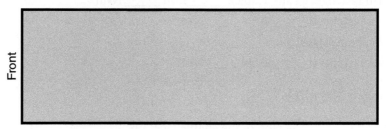

Front

Figure 32-2. Draw the bolt arrangement for the head you are working on. Write the sequence number of each bolt. If you are working on a V-type engine, draw the tightening sequence for one head.

Project 9: Job 32 *(continued)*

☐ 7. Torque the head bolts to three-fourths of the full torque specification. Follow the correct tightening sequence.

What is three-fourths of the head bolt torque specification?

_____

☐ 8. Tighten the head bolts to the full torque value following the correct tightening sequence. Then, recheck each bolt to ensure that all are at full torque.

What is the full head bolt torque specification?

_____

Did any of the bolts turn when you tightened them for the final time? Yes ___ No ___

If Yes, can you think of a reason that some of the bolts could be turned more?

_____

☐ 9. If the engine has an overhead camshaft that can only be installed after the head bolts have been installed and torqued, install the camshaft now. Refer to the following procedure:

 a. Lubricate the cam journals.

 b. Install the cam bearings, if used.

 c. Place the camshaft in position.

 d. Place the bearing caps in position.

 e. Check bearing clearances with Plastigage as needed. This may require temporarily performing substep f.

 f. Install the rocker arm shafts if they are part of the bearing cap assembly. Tighten the fasteners one-half turn at a time, starting with the middle bolts. Remember that the compressed valve springs will be pushing against the rocker shaft.

 g. Torque the cap bolts to specifications.

 h. If the camshaft has a timing advance mechanism, install it now.

 i. If the head has two camshafts, repeat substeps a through h for the other camshaft.

Note: This completes head installation. Some manufacturers recommend that the head bolts be retorqued after the engine has been started and has reached full operating temperature. The instructions with the new head gaskets will normally provide this information.

☐ 10. If the engine is a V-type, repeat steps 2 through 9 for the other head.

Install Lifters, Push Rods, Rocker Arms, and Valve Cover(s)

Note: Not all of the following steps will apply to every engine. This procedure assumes that, if the engine has an in-block camshaft, the camshaft has been previously installed. If the rocker arms and shaft(s) were installed earlier, skip steps 1 and 2.

☐ 1. Install the lifters in their original locations.

☐ 2. Install the push rods and rocker arms in their original locations. If a rocker shaft is used, start the rocker shaft fasteners by hand. Then, tighten the fasteners, starting with the middle bolts and turning each bolt one-half turn at a time. This will prevent a strain on any one bolt. Remember, the pressure of the compressed valve springs will be pushing against the rocker shaft assembly.

 Note: On some engines, the valves may need adjusting at this time. See Job 29.

☐ 3. If the valves do not have to be readjusted after the engine is started, install the valve covers. Use new gaskets and torque the fasteners to specification.

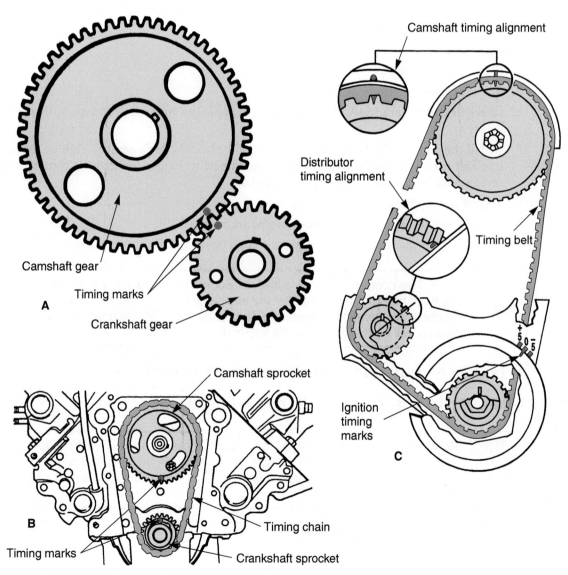

Figure 32-3. Three types of timing mechanisms are shown here. A—Gear-driven timing mechanism. B—Chain-driven timing mechanism. C—Belt-driven timing mechanism. (Chrysler, Ford)

Name _____

Install the Valve Timing Components and Front Cover

☐ 1. Loosely place the timing gears or sprockets on the crankshaft and camshaft and rotate the crankshaft and camshaft until the timing marks are aligned. **Figure 32-3** illustrates the three types of timing mechanisms.

☐ 2. Carefully remove the sprockets or gears, ensuring the crankshaft and camshaft do not turn.

☐ 3. Place the timing chain or belt in position over the sprockets. Be careful to maintain the alignment of the timing marks. **Figure 32-4** shows common alignment marks for chain and belt type timing gears.

☐ 4. Install the sprockets and chain or belt into position on the camshaft and crankshaft. Be careful not to allow the crankshaft or camshaft to rotate.

☐ 5. Install and tighten the timing device fasteners.

☐ 6. Check and adjust belt/chain tension using one of the following methods, as outlined by the manufacturer's instructions:

> **Note:** On many engines, belt or chain tension is not adjustable.

- Measure belt deflection with a special tool and adjust the tensioner as required. Adjustment devices include slotted holes in the tensioner, adjusting screws, or shims.
- Adjust the tensioner until the belt can be twisted to a 90° angle.
- Use a torque wrench to adjust the tensioner to the proper torque value.
- Align marks on the tensioner with marks on the engine block or head.

Method used:

_____

A   B

Figure 32-4. Make sure that the timing gears are correctly aligned before completing assembly. A—The timing marks on this chain and timing gear assembly are correctly aligned. B—Mark the timing belt sprockets with a tire crayon or other durable marker before installing them.

☐ 7. After all parts are installed, recheck the timing marks to ensure that they are in position.

☐ 8. Index the camshaft position sensor using manufacturer's procedures. On most engines, the camshaft and crankshaft position sensors are indexed by the following procedure:

    a. Place the sensor in position on the engine block or timing cover and lightly attach the fasteners.

    b. Ensure that the marks on the camshaft position sensor are aligned with the marks on the engine block or timing cover.

    c. Tighten the fasteners, being sure that the marks remain in alignment.

☐ 9. Scrape the timing cover, coolant pump, and block mating surfaces to remove old gasket material. Install a new front seal in the timing cover.

☐ 10. Place the timing cover gaskets and seals on the engine block. Use the proper type of sealant, if required.

☐ 11. Place the timing cover on the block. Be careful not to damage the new seal.

☐ 12. Install and tighten the timing cover fasteners. Tighten the fasteners to the proper torque in the correct sequence.

Job Wrap-Up

☐ 1. Clean and return all of the tools and clean the work area.

☐ 2. Did you encounter any problems during this procedure? Yes ___ No ___
If Yes, describe the problems:

_____

_____

What did you do to correct the problems?

_____

_____

☐ 3. Have your instructor check your work and sign this job sheet.

Performance Evaluation—Instructor Use Only

Did the student complete the job in the time allotted? Yes ___ No ___

If No, which steps were not completed? _____

How would you rate this student's overall performance on this job? _____

5–Excellent, 4–Good, 3–Satisfactory, 2–Unsatisfactory, 1–Poor

Comments: _____

_____

_____

INSTRUCTOR'S SIGNATURE_____

Project 9:   Job 33—Complete the Engine Reassembly

After completing this job, you will be able to install the remaining engine components onto a long block to prepare it for reinstallation into the vehicle.

Instructions

As you read the job instructions, answer the questions and perform the tasks. Record your answers using complete sentences. Consult the proper service literature and ask your instructor for help as needed.

> **⚠ Warning:** Before performing this job, review all pertinent safety information in the text and discuss safety procedures with your instructor.

Procedures

> **Note:** This job assumes that the engine has been reassembled to the long block stage. Refer to Job 31 for instructions for assembling an engine to the short block stage and Job 32 for procedures for assembling an engine to the long block stage.

☐ 1. Obtain an engine to be used in this job. Your instructor may direct you to perform this job on a shop engine.

- Make of engine:

_____

- Number of cylinders:

_____

- Cylinder arrangement (V-type, inline, etc.):

_____

- Cooling system: Liquid ____ Air ____

☐ 2. Gather the tools needed to perform the following tasks. Refer to the tools and materials list at the beginning of the project.

Install the Intake Manifold

☐ 1. Install the intake manifold gaskets. Use sealer on the ends of the gasket if recommended by the manufacturer, **Figure 33-1**.

> **Note:** On some inline engines, the intake and exhaust manifolds are installed together.

☐ 2. Place the intake manifold in position on the engine.

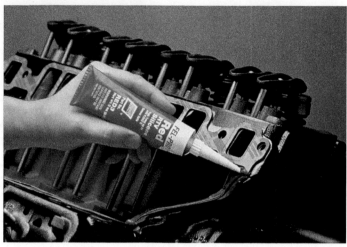

Figure 33-1. If called for by the manufacturer, use sealer at the corner of the gaskets at the points where separate head and block gaskets butt against each other. Use the correct type of sealer to avoid leaks. (Fel-Pro)

☐ 3. Install all intake manifold fasteners hand tight.

☐ 4. Determine whether there is a tightening sequence for the intake manifold bolts.

Did you find a tightening sequence for the manifold bolts? Yes ___ No ___

If Yes, draw the sequence in **Figure 33-2**.

If there is no sequence, begin at the center and alternate sides, tightening outward.

☐ 5. Tighten the intake manifold bolts, in the prescribed sequence, to one-half of the full torque specification.

What is one-half of the torque specification?

_____

☐ 6. Tighten the intake manifold bolts, in the prescribed sequence, to three-fourths of the full torque specification.

What is three-fourths of the head bolt torque specification?

_____

☐ 7. Torque the intake manifold bolts to the full torque specification following the correct sequence.

A

B

Figure 33-2. Draw the manifold bolt arrangement and write the sequence number of each bolt. A—Use this pattern for a V-type engine. B—Use this pattern for an inline engine.

Project 9: Job 33 *(continued)*

☐ 8. Following the prescribed tightening sequence, recheck each manifold fastener to ensure that all are at full torque.

What is the full torque specification?

_____

Did any of the fasteners turn when you tightened them for the final time? Yes ___ No ___

Can you think of a reason that some of the fasteners could be turned more?

_____

_____

Note: Some manufacturers recommend retightening the bolts after the engine is warmed to operating temperature and allowed to cool.

Install the Exhaust Manifold(s)

☐ 1. Position the exhaust manifold(s) on the head, using gaskets where applicable.

☐ 2. Install all exhaust manifold fasteners hand tight.

☐ 3. Tighten the bolts to the proper torque specification, following the prescribed sequence or beginning at the center and alternating outward.

Torque:

_____

Complete the Engine Reassembly

☐ 1. Replace the coolant pump gasket and place the coolant pump on the block or timing cover, as applicable.

☐ 2. Install and tighten the pump fasteners to the proper torque in the proper sequence.

☐ 3. If the engine is equipped with a mechanical fuel pump, reinstall it now. Be sure to use a new gasket.

☐ 4. Install the vibration damper. If the vibration damper has a rotor for use with a crankshaft position sensor, align the rotor and sensor with the necessary special tool.

☐ 5. Place the flywheel on the crankshaft flange.

Note: Flywheel installation may have to wait until after the engine is removed from the engine stand.

☐ 6. Install and tighten the flywheel bolts. These bolts *must* be torqued correctly.

Torque:

_____

Note: If the vehicle has a manual transmission or transaxle, install the clutch and pressure plate. Use a pilot shaft during installation to ensure that the clutch disc is properly positioned.

☐ 7. If the valves do not have to be readjusted after the engine is started, install the valve covers if they are not already installed.

☐ 8. Install the turbocharger or supercharger, if used.

☐ 9. Install any remaining engine parts. If the engine has a distributor, time it to the engine during installation.

> **Caution:** Some engines have a camshaft position sensor and a distributor-mounted crankshaft position sensor. The relationship of these sensors must be checked and adjusted. Failure to make this adjustment may cause random misfires, MIL illumination, or failure to start. The distributor housing may have an indexing mark for proper positioning. On other engines, a scan tool or a dual trace lab scope may be needed to determine the relative sensor positions with the engine running or being cranked. Adjustment is made by turning the distributor housing.

> **Note:** At this point, the engine is ready to be reinstalled in the vehicle, as described in Job 34.

Job Wrap-Up

☐ 1. Clean and return all of the tools and clean the work area.

☐ 2. Did you encounter any problems during this procedure? Yes ____ No ____
If Yes, describe the problems:

_____

_____

What did you do to correct the problems?

_____

_____

☐ 3. Have your instructor check your work and sign this job sheet.

Performance Evaluation—Instructor Use Only

Did the student complete the job in the time allotted? Yes ____ No ____

If No, which steps were not completed? _____

How would you rate this student's overall performance on this job? _____

5–Excellent, 4–Good, 3–Satisfactory, 2–Unsatisfactory, 1–Poor

Comments: _____

_____

_____

INSTRUCTOR'S SIGNATURE_____

Project 9: Job 34—Reinstall the Engine

After completing this job, you will be able to install and properly reconnect a vehicle's engine.

Instructions

As you read the job instructions, answer the questions and perform the tasks. Record your answers using complete sentences. Consult the proper service literature and ask your instructor for help as needed.

 Warning: Before performing this job, review all pertinent safety information in the text and discuss safety procedures with your instructor.

Procedures

1. Obtain a vehicle and engine to be used in this job. Your instructor may direct you to perform this job on a shop vehicle and engine.

2. Gather the tools needed to perform the following job. Refer to the tools and materials list at the beginning of the project.

3. Attach the lifting chain to the engine as was done to remove it. Be sure that the chain is securely attached. Lift the engine enough to remove tension on the holding fixture. Remove any bolts securing the engine to the holding fixture and then carefully lift the engine.

4. Install the flywheel, if it is not already installed. Refer to Job 33.

5. Lower the engine into position in the engine compartment, **Figure 34-1**.

6. Align the engine with the transmission or transaxle. **Figure 34-2** shows the engine and transmission being brought into alignment.

Figure 34-1. The engine may have to be tilted at an angle to allow it to enter the engine compartment.

Figure 34-2. Align the engine and transmission before tightening any fasteners. A jack had to be placed under the oil pan to align this engine and transmission.

 Caution: If the vehicle has a manual transmission or transaxle, be extremely careful to align the clutch disc with the input shaft. Misalignment could result in serious clutch damage.

☐ 7. If the vehicle has an automatic transmission or transaxle, ensure that the flywheel and torque converter are in the same relative position, and that the converter is not binding against the flywheel. If the converter is attached to the flywheel through studs, make sure that the studs pass through the flywheel before proceeding to the next steps. See **Figure 34-3**.

☐ 8. Install the fasteners holding the transmission or transaxle to the engine.

☐ 9. Install and tighten the engine mount fasteners and remove the lifting fixture.

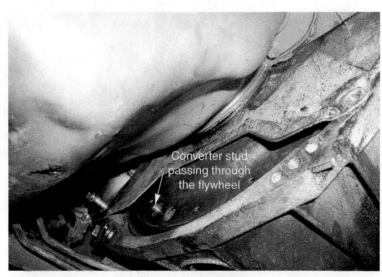

Figure 34-3. Be sure that the converter studs pass through the correct holes in the flywheel before continuing the installation.

Project 9: Job 31 *(continued)*

- [ ] 10. Install and tighten the flywheel-to-torque converter fasteners.
- [ ] 11. Install the starter and reattach the starter wires.
- [ ] 12. Install the flywheel cover and any engine-to-transmission brackets.
- [ ] 13. Reattach the exhaust system.
- [ ] 14. Install the vacuum lines on the intake manifold.
- [ ] 15. Install the fuel lines.
- [ ] 16. Install the throttle linkage and any related linkages.
- [ ] 17. Install the air cleaner assembly or air inlet ducts.
- [ ] 18. Install the power steering pump, if used.
- [ ] 19. Install the air conditioner compressor, if used.
- [ ] 20. Install any belts and tighten them to specifications.
- [ ] 21. Install all electrical connectors and ground straps.
- [ ] 22. Install the radiator and heater hoses.
- [ ] 23. Refill the cooling system with the proper type of coolant.
- [ ] 24. Add the proper type of engine oil until the level reaches the full mark on the dipstick.
- [ ] 25. Reconnect the battery negative cable.
- [ ] 26. If the vehicle has an electric fuel pump, turn the ignition switch to the *On* position and allow the fuel system to refill.
- [ ] 27. Check the fluid level in the power steering and transmission or transaxle. Add the proper type of fluid as needed.
- [ ] 28. Start the engine.
- [ ] 29. Check for proper engine operation and leaks as the engine warms up. Make any necessary ignition or fuel system adjustments.
- [ ] 30. Reinstall the hood.
- [ ] 31. Road test the vehicle to ensure that all repairs are satisfactory.

Job Wrap-Up

- [ ] 1. Clean the work area and return any equipment to storage.
- [ ] 2. Did you encounter any problems during this procedure? Yes ___ No ___
   If Yes, describe the problems:

   _____

   _____

   What did you do to correct the problems?

   _____

   _____

- [ ] 3. Have your instructor check your work and sign this job sheet.

Performance Evaluation—Instructor Use Only

Did the student complete the job in the time allotted? Yes ___ No ___

If No, which steps were not completed? _____

How would you rate this student's overall performance on this job? _____

5–Excellent, 4–Good, 3–Satisfactory, 2–Unsatisfactory, 1–Poor

Comments: _____

_____

_____

INSTRUCTOR'S SIGNATURE_____

Project 10

Servicing a Cooling System

Introduction

The cooling system removes about one-third of the heat produced by the engine. If the cooling system is neglected, the engine can overheat and be damaged in a short time. Lack of cooling system maintenance can affect vehicle drivability and heater operation.

The cooling system consists of many components, all of which can fail. While modern vehicles are designed to require less maintenance, they also last for many more years than they did previously, so the chance of encountering a defective cooling system part remains the same. If defective cooling system parts are not replaced, the engine can overheat and be destroyed.

As you work through the jobs in this project, you will perform periodic maintenance and replace faulty or worn parts in a cooling system. In Job 35, you will inspect and perform diagnostic tests on a cooling system. You will flush and bleed the cooling system in Job 36. In Job 37, you will replace cooling system belts and hoses. You will replace a vehicle's coolant pump in Job 38, and a vehicle's radiator in Job 39. In Job 40, you will remove and replace a vehicle's thermostat.

Project 10 Jobs

- Job 35—Inspect and Test a Cooling System
- Job 36—Flush and Bleed a Cooling System
- Job 37—Replace Belts and Hoses
- Job 38—Replace a Coolant Pump
- Job 39—Replace a Radiator
- Job 40—Remove and Replace a Thermostat

Tools and Materials

The following list contains the tools and materials that may be needed to complete the jobs in this project. The items used will depend on the make and model of the vehicle being serviced.

- Vehicle in need of cooling system service.
- Applicable service information.
- Cooling system pressure tester.
- Hydrometer or other type of coolant tester.

- Temperature tester.
- Drain pan(s).
- Hand tools.
- Air-powered tools.
- Safety glasses and other protective equipment.

Safety Notice

Before performing these jobs, review all pertinent safety information in the text and review safety information with your instructor.

Project 10: Job 35—Inspect and Test a Cooling System

After completing this job, you will be able to inspect a cooling system and diagnose cooling system problems.

Instructions

As you read the job instructions, answer the questions and perform the tasks. Record your answers using complete sentences. Consult the proper service literature and ask your instructor for help as needed.

> ⚠ **Warning:** Before performing this job, review all pertinent safety information in the text and discuss safety procedures with your instructor.

Procedures

☐ 1. Obtain a vehicle on which cooling system service can be performed. Your instructor may direct you to perform this job on a shop vehicle.

☐ 2. Gather the tools needed to perform the following job. Refer to the tools and materials list at the beginning of the project.

☐ 3. Determine the type of antifreeze to be used in the vehicle cooling system.

Antifreeze type:

_____

Inspect for Non-Cooling System Causes of Overheating

☐ 1. Inspect the vehicle and operating conditions for the following:
- Radiator blocked by debris or front body modifications: Yes ___ No ___
- Missing air dam below front bumper: Yes ___ No ___
- Restricted exhaust system (refer to Job 8 for testing procedures): Yes ___ No ___
- Binding or resistance in drive train: Yes ___ No ___
- Dragging brakes or other resistance in brake system: Yes___ No ___
- Excessive idling, especially in gear and/or with the air conditioning operating: Yes ___ No ___
- Operating at extreme high speed: Yes ___ No ___
- Towing or other extra weight situation: Yes ___ No ___
- Extreme ambient temperatures: Yes ___ No ___

If Yes, describe the problem(s):

_____

_____

Inspect Belts and Hoses

☐ 1. Open the hood and visually inspect the condition of the cooling system hoses. Examine the hoses for bulges, leaks, or deterioration (such as frayed areas). Ensure that the hoses do not contact any moving parts. Squeeze the hoses to check for hardness, cracks, or softness, **Figure 35-1**.

Figure 35-1. Squeeze the hose to determine whether it is excessively soft. Be careful when doing this on a warmed up engine as the hose will be hot.

Are any problems found? Yes ___ No ___

If Yes, describe the problems:

_____

_____

☐ 2. Determine the condition of the vehicle's belts. Examine the belts for glazing, fraying, or oil contamination. Note whether the belts are loose by attempting to turn the pulley on one of the accessories with the engine off. If applicable, note the condition of the belt tensioner.

Are any problems found? Yes ___ No ___

If Yes, describe the problems:

_____

_____

☐ 3. Inspect the belt tensioner for the following defects:

- Weak tensioner spring resistance.

- Worn pulley grooves.

- Worn bearings (roughness when turning the tensioner).

Can the tensioner be reused? Yes ___ No ___

If No, explain:

_____

_____

☐ 4. Check the pulley alignment of the belt system(s). Sight along the pulleys to ensure that they are properly aligned, as shown in **Figure 35-2**.

Are the pulleys and belts aligned? Yes ___ No ___

If No, describe the relative positions of the pulleys:

_____

_____

Inspect Other Cooling System Components

☐ 1. Visually check the radiator's condition. Make sure the radiator fins are free of leaves or other debris and are not damaged. Also, check for obvious leaks.

Are any problems found? Yes ___ No ___

Project 10: Job 35 *(continued)*

Figure 35-2. The easiest way to determine whether the pulleys and belts are aligned is to make a visual check. Note the alignment of the various pulleys and the belt in this figure.

If Yes, describe the problems:

_____

_____

☐ 2. Check the condition of the coolant recovery system. Inspect the coolant recovery tank, cap, and hoses for damage. Inspect the coolant in the tank for excessive rust and discoloration. This can be done visually, as shown in **Figure 35-3**.

Are any problems found? Yes ___ No ___

If Yes, describe the problems:

_____

_____

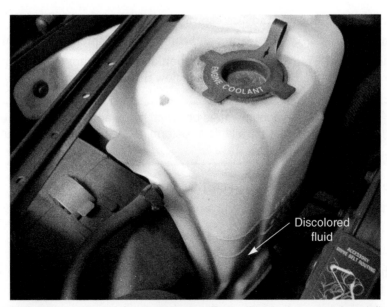

Figure 35-3. Visually check the reservoir for discoloration. Rust will stain the reservoir and discolor the coolant.

☐ 3. Ensure that the engine and cooling system are sufficiently cool (cooling system not under pressure) to allow the radiator cap to be safely removed.

☐ 4. Remove the radiator cap and check its condition. Replace the cap if it is corroded or if the rubber seal is hard, cracked, or otherwise damaged.

   Is the cap in good condition? Yes ___ No ___

☐ 5. Check the coolant level in the radiator. If the cooling system has a coolant recovery system, the coolant level should be at the top of the filler neck. If the vehicle does not have a coolant recovery system, the coolant level should about 3″ (75 mm) below the filler neck.

   Is the coolant level correct? Yes ___ No ___

   If No, add coolant to bring the fluid level to the proper level.

☐ 6. Visually check the coolant for rust.

   Is the coolant rusty? Yes ___ No ___

   If Yes, the cooling system should be flushed.

☐ 7. Check the degree of freeze protection (antifreeze percentage) with a coolant tester. Follow the directions provided by the tester manufacturer.

   Antifreeze will protect to _____ °F or °C (circle one).

Pressure Test the Pressure Cap

☐ 1. Obtain a cooling system pressure tester.

☐ 2. Check the condition of the radiator cap. Install the cap on the tester, **Figure 35-4**. Adapters may be needed to properly test the cap. Pump up the tester pressure until it levels off. A pressure specification should be printed somewhere on the cap. The radiator cap should hold this pressure without allowing it to drop.

   Does the radiator cap pass the pressure test? Yes ___ No ___

   If No, replace the radiator cap.

Vacuum Test the Pressure Cap

☐ 1. Obtain a vacuum pump and radiator cap vacuum test adapter.

☐ 2. Install the pressure cap on the adapter and connect the adapter to the vacuum pump.

☐ 3. Apply vacuum to the radiator cap. The cap should allow vacuum to build up to approximately 2″ Hg to 5″ Hg, then release and allow air to flow through the cap.

Note: Release vacuum varies between manufacturers. Check the specifications when available to determine the proper release vacuum for a particular vehicle.

   Does the cap allow vacuum to build up, then release? Yes ___ No ___

   If No, replace the radiator cap.

Pressure Test the Cooling System

☐ 1. Install the pressure tester on the radiator filler neck. See **Figure 35-5**. If the system is very low on coolant, first add coolant to make the job of pressurizing easier.

Name_____

Figure 35-4. Install the pressure cap on the pressure tester. Adapters may be needed, as shown here. (Jack Klasey)

Figure 35-5. Install the pressure tester on the radiator filler neck. (Jack Klasey)

☐ 2. Pump up the pressure tester until the cooling system has been pressurized to the rating on the radiator cap. Carefully observe the cooling system for leaks. If no leaks are visible and the pressure holds for two minutes, the system is not leaking.

Does the cooling system pass the pressure test? Yes ___ No ___

If No, explain why the cooling system failed:

_____

_____

_____

 Caution: If you add water to the cooling system for diagnostic testing, make sure you drain the system and refill it with the proper antifreeze-water mixture before releasing the vehicle to its owner.

Make Visual Checks for Leaks

☐ 1. Check all visible gaskets, fittings, and freeze plugs for the presence of coolant.
Describe any leaks or suspicious areas:

_____

_____

☐ 2. Check all engine surfaces for pools of coolant.
Are there pools of coolant on any of the engine surfaces? Yes ____ No ____
If Yes, describe the location:

_____

Based on your visual inspection, does the engine have leaks that must be corrected?
Yes ____ No ____
If Yes, consult your instructor about the needed repairs.

☐ 3. Check the front floorboards and under the dash for any signs of coolant leaks. Any coolant found under the dash or on the floorboard likely indicates a leaking heater core. Also, check for leaks at the heater hose connections.
Were any leaks found? Yes ____ No ____.
If Yes, describe:

_____

_____

_____

Note: If a suspected leak proves to be difficult to locate, fluorescent dye can be added to the coolant. After the coolant has been warmed and circulated, any leaking coolant will glow brightly when a UV light is shined on it.

Check the Coolant Pump

☐ 1. Check the coolant pump for leaks at the gaskets and weep hole. The weep hole is usually located on the housing between the pulley flange and the rear of the pump.
Do you find any leaks? Yes ____ No ____
If Yes, consult your instructor about the needed repairs.

Note: It is normal for a slight amount of coolant to be present at the weep hole.

Belt-Driven Pump

☐ 1. Check the pump bearings for wear by attempting to move the pump shaft up and down and back and forth. There should be almost no movement.
Do you detect excessive movement? Yes ____ No ____
If Yes, consult your instructor about the needed repairs.

Name _____

Electric Motor–Driven Pump

☐   1. Ensure that the pump motor runs whenever the ignition switch is in the *On* position.

      Does the pump motor operate with the ignition switch in the *On* position? Yes ___ No ___

      If No, consult your instructor about needed repairs.

Check Coolant Temperature and Cooling Fan Operation

☐   1. Ensure that the vehicle cooling system is full.

☐   2. Replace the radiator cap if it was removed.

☐   3. Start the vehicle and allow it to warm up. If the vehicle has an air conditioner, turn it on to shorten the warm up time.

☐   4. As the engine warms up, periodically check the engine temperature and record it in the spaces provided. Circle the temperature scale used, °F or °C.

      One minute after startup: _____ °F or °C

      Three minutes after startup: _____ °F or °C

      Five minutes after startup: _____ °F or °C

      Ten minutes after startup (if necessary): _____ °F or °C

Electric Cooling Fan

☐   1. Observe the cooling fan. It should come on shortly after the engine reaches operating temperature. On some vehicles, the fan will come on when the air conditioner high-side pressure reaches a certain value, or it may run whenever the air conditioner is on. Many vehicles have two cooling fans. One or both fans will come on as the engine warms up.

      Does the fan come on when needed? Yes ___ No ___

      If No, consult your instructor for further instructions.

Belt-Driven Fan and Fan Clutch

☐   1. Observe the cooling fan air flow. It should be pulling air through the radiator when the engine is at operating temperature.

> **Note:** Consult your instructor if you are not sure whether the fan is pulling enough air through the radiator.

☐   2. Stop the engine while observing the fan. The fan should stop turning within one revolution.

      Does the fan stop within one revolution? Yes ___ No ___

      If No, consult your instructor for further instructions.

Check Fan Shroud and Air Dams

☐   1. Visually inspect the fan shroud for the following problems:
- Cracks.
- Missing parts.
- Loose or missing shroud fasteners.
- Evidence that the fan is hitting the shroud.

☐ 2. Visually inspect the air dams for the following problems:
  - Tears or cracks.
  - Missing dams.
  - Loose or missing dam fasteners.

  Do you observe any of the above problems? Yes ___ No ___

  If Yes, consult your instructor for further instructions.

Check for Combustion Leaks

Note: Due to the variation in types of combustion testers, the following steps outline only a general method of combustion testing.

☐ 1. Ensure that the vehicle's cooling system is full.
☐ 2. Check that the cooling system is *not* under pressure and then remove the radiator cap.
☐ 3. Install the combustion tester on the filler neck.
☐ 4. Start the engine and follow the manufacturer's directions to test for the presence of combustion gases in the cooling system.

  Are combustion gases detected in the cooling system? Yes ___ No ___

  If Yes, consult your instructor for further instructions before continuing.

☐ 5. Remove the tester and replace the radiator cap.

Inspect the Engine Oil Cooler

☐ 1. If the vehicle has an auxiliary engine oil cooler, check it for the following problems:
  - Visible leaks.
  - Clogged fins.
  - Cracked, damaged, or loose hoses or lines.

  Are any problems found? Yes ___ No ___

  If Yes, describe the problems:

  _____

  _____

☐ 2. Clean up any spilled coolant.

Name _____

Job Wrap-Up

☐   1. Clean the work area and return any equipment to storage.

☐   2. Did you encounter any problems during this procedure? Yes ___ No ___
      If Yes, describe the problems:

_____

_____

      What did you do to correct the problems?

_____

_____

☐   3. Have your instructor check your work and sign this job sheet.

Performance Evaluation—Instructor Use Only

Did the student complete the job in the time allotted? Yes ___ No ___

If No, which steps were not completed? _____

How would you rate this student's overall performance on this job? _____

5–Excellent, 4–Good, 3–Satisfactory, 2–Unsatisfactory, 1–Poor

Comments: _____

_____

_____

INSTRUCTOR'S SIGNATURE _____

Notes

Project 10: Job 36—Flush and Bleed a Cooling System

After completing this job, you will be able to flush and bleed a cooling system.

Instructions

As you read the job instructions, answer the questions and perform the tasks. Record your answers using complete sentences. Consult the proper service literature and ask your instructor for help as needed.

> ⚠ **Warning:** Before performing this job, review all pertinent safety information in the text and discuss safety procedures with your instructor.

Procedures

☐ 1. Obtain a vehicle on which cooling system service can be performed. Your instructor may direct you to perform this job on a shop vehicle.

☐ 2. Gather the tools needed to perform the following job. Refer to the project's tools and materials list.

☐ 3. Determine the type of antifreeze to be used in the vehicle's cooling system.

Antifreeze type:

_____

> 📋 **Note:** Many shops have pressure flushing and refilling machines. To use such a machine, use the manufacturer's procedures rather than the steps given here.

☐ 4. Ensure that the engine and cooling system are sufficiently cool (cooling system not under pressure) to allow the radiator cap to be safely removed.

☐ 5. Remove the radiator cap, then locate the radiator drain plug. Locate any coolant drain plugs on the engine.

> 📋 **Note:** Some coolant recovery tanks are pressurized. Relieve system pressure by loosening the cap on the recovery tank before removing the radiator cap, **Figure 36-1**.

☐ 6. Place a suitable container under the drain plug(s).

☐ 7. Open the radiator drain plug and any coolant drain plugs on the engine. Make sure that coolant drains into the containers.

> ⚠ **Warning:** Clean up any coolant spills. Antifreeze is poisonous to people and animals.

Figure 36-1. If the recovery tank is pressurized, loosen the tank cap before removing the radiator cap.

☐ 8. Allow the coolant to drain into the container(s) until coolant stops coming from the drain plugs.

☐ 9. Close the drain plugs.

☐ 10. Refill the cooling system with water and flushing agent. Carefully follow the directions provided by the manufacturer of the flushing agent.

☐ 11. Start the engine and allow it to idle for the recommended time. Turn the vehicle heater to high and closely monitor the level in the radiator.

☐ 12. After the recommended time has elapsed, turn the engine off.

☐ 13. Open the drain plugs and observe the water as it drains.

Did the water come out clear? Yes ___ No ___

If Yes, skip ahead to step 16.

☐ 14. Close the drain plugs and refill the system with water.

☐ 15. Repeat steps 11 through 14 until the water from the drain plugs is clear. The length of this procedure varies depending on the condition of the cooling system and the number of times the cooling system must be flushed to remove all of the cleaning agent.

☐ 16. Make sure the drain plugs are closed. Refill the cooling system with a 50-50 mixture of the proper type of antifreeze and clean water.

What type of antifreeze does this engine require?

_____

Caution: Many modern vehicles take special long-life coolant. Always install the proper type of coolant. Do *not* mix coolant types.

☐ 17. Bleed the system using one of the following procedures, depending on the relative placement of the engine and radiator.

- **Radiator higher than engine:** Fill the system to about 3″ (76 mm) below the top of the filler neck. Allow the engine to reach operating temperature. When the thermostat opens, the radiator level will drop. Add more coolant until the level is at the top of the filler neck (coolant recovery system) or 3″ (76 mm) below the filler neck (no coolant recovery system).

Project 10: Job 36 (continued)

- **Engine higher than radiator:** Fill the system to about 3″ (76 mm) below the top of the filler neck. Allow the engine to reach operating temperature. When the thermostat opens, the radiator level will drop. Open the bleed valve(s) on the engine, **Figure 36-2**, and add more coolant until the coolant begins exit from the bleed valve. Close the bleed valve and add coolant to fill the radiator. On some vehicles, the bleeder may need to be opened and closed several times to remove all air from the system.

☐ 18. Install the radiator cap.

☐ 19. Add coolant to the cold level on the coolant recovery reservoir.

☐ 20. Clean up any spilled coolant.

Figure 36-2. Some vehicles have two bleed valves on opposite sides of the engine. Both should be used to remove all air from the cooling system.

Job Wrap-Up

☐ 1. Clean the work area and return any equipment to storage.

☐ 2. Did you encounter any problems during this procedure? Yes ___ No ___
   If Yes, describe the problems:

   _____

   _____

   What did you do to correct the problems?

   _____

   _____

☐ 3. Have your instructor check your work and sign this job sheet.

Performance Evaluation—Instructor Use Only

Did the student complete the job in the time allotted? Yes ___ No ___

If No, which steps were not completed? _____

How would you rate this student's overall performance on this job?_____

5–Excellent, 4–Good, 3–Satisfactory, 2–Unsatisfactory, 1–Poor

Comments: _____

_____

_____

INSTRUCTOR'S SIGNATURE_____

Project 10: Job 37—Replace Belts and Hoses

After completing this job, you will be able to replace V-belts, serpentine belts, radiator hoses, and heater hoses.

Instructions

As you read the job instructions, answer the questions and perform the tasks. Record your answers using complete sentences. Consult the proper service literature and ask your instructor for help as needed.

> ⚠ **Warning:** Before performing this job, review all pertinent safety information in the text and discuss safety procedures with your instructor.

Procedures

☐ 1. Obtain a vehicle to be used in this job. Your instructor may direct you to perform this job on a shop vehicle.

☐ 2. Gather the tools needed to perform the following job. Refer to the tools and materials list at the beginning of the project.

Replace a V-Belt

☐ 1. Determine which belt must be replaced. V-belts are used to drive combinations of accessories, including the coolant pump, alternator, air conditioning compressor, power steering pump, and air pump. Some or all of these accessories must be loosened to remove a particular belt. Sometimes one or more serviceable belts must be removed to remove the defective belt.

Which accessories are driven by the belt that will be replaced?

_____

_____

☐ 2. Loosen the fasteners holding the accessory driven by the belt. You may need a droplight so that you can find all of the fasteners. **Figure 37-1** illustrates accessory slotted and pivot points.

☐ 3. Push the accessory toward the engine to remove tension on the belt.

☐ 4. Remove the belt from the pulleys.

☐ 5. Compare the old and new belts.

Is the new belt the correct replacement? Yes ___ No ___

> **Note:** Even a slight difference in size means that the new belt is unusable.

☐ 6. Slip the new belt over the pulleys, making sure that it is fully seated in the pulley grooves.

☐ 7. Pull the accessories away from the engine to place slight tension on the belt.

☐ 8. Adjust belt tension. Use a belt tension gauge to measure exact tension. If a gauge is not available, use the belt deflection method to adjust the belt. The belt should deflect from 1/2″ to 5/8″ (13 mm to 16 mm) with 25 pounds (10 kg) of applied pressure. The belts should only be tight enough to

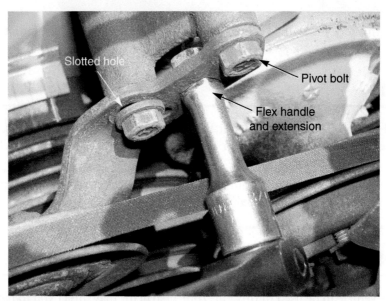

Figure 37-1. A slotted hole and pivot point arrangement provides for V-belt adjustment. The bolt passing through the slotted hole is loosened, allowing the accessory to be rotated around the pivot bolt to tension or loosen the belt. In the arrangement shown here, a square hole is provided in the bracket so a 1/2″ ratchet or flex handle can be used to reposition the accessory.

prevent slipping or squealing. Excessive tension on the belt places undo stress on the accessory bearings, which will quickly wear out.

☐ 9. Start the vehicle and check belt operation.

Replace a Serpentine Belt

 Note: This procedure assumes that the vehicle has one serpentine belt. If you must remove other belts in order to replace the serpentine belt, use this procedure to remove serpentine belts or the previous procedure to remove V-belts.

☐ 1. Open the vehicle hood and determine whether the engine contains a label showing serpentine belt routing, or obtain service literature showing serpentine belt routing for the vehicle on which you are working.

☐ 2. Locate the belt-tensioning device and determine which tool(s) are needed to remove tension. This may be simple hand tools or a special tool, **Figure 37-2**.

Tool(s) needed to remove tension:

_____

☐ 3. Remove tension from the belt using the proper tool(s).

☐ 4. Remove the serpentine belt.

☐ 5. Slowly release the belt-tensioning device.

☐ 6. Turn the pulley of the belt-tensioning device.

Is any roughness noted? Yes ___ No ___

If Yes, the pulley should be replaced. Consult your instructor before proceeding.

Name_____

Figure 37-2. Serpentine belt tension can usually be removed by inserting a 3/8″ or 1/2″ ratchet or flex handle into a square hole in the tensioner and pulling away from the direction of tension. Sometimes a special tool is needed to remove belt tension.

☐ 7. Compare the old and new belts.
Are the belts the same size? Yes ___ No ___
If No, obtain the correct belt before proceeding.

☐ 8. Refer to the proper belt routing diagram and place the new belt in position.

☐ 9. Pull the belt-tensioning device away from the belt to allow the belt to be installed.

☐ 10. Finish installing the new belt, making sure that the belt is properly positioned over the pulleys.

☐ 11. Slowly release the belt-tensioning device.

☐ 12. Start the engine and check belt operation.

Remove and Replace Cooling System and Heater Hoses

☐ 1. Determine which hose(s) must be replaced.
Hose(s) to replace:

_____

☐ 2. Ensure that the engine and cooling system are sufficiently cool (cooling system not under pressure) to allow the radiator cap to be safely removed.

☐ 3. Remove the radiator cap, then locate the radiator drain plug.

☐ 4. Place a suitable container under the drain plug.

☐ 5. Open the radiator drain plug. Ensure that coolant drains into the container.

⚠️ **Warning:** Clean up any coolant spills. Antifreeze is poisonous to people and animals.

6. Allow the coolant to drain out so that the level of coolant in the engine is below the level of the hose nipples. It is not necessary to remove all of the coolant unless the lower radiator hose is being replaced.

7. Loosen and remove the hose clamps. Most modern vehicles use spring clamps (sometimes called "hog ring" clamps), which can be removed by compressing the spring tabs with a pair of pliers, **Figure 37-3**.

8. Remove the hose. It may be necessary to split the hose at the hose nipple to make removal easier.

> **Caution:** Be careful not to damage the hose nipples. These can easily be deformed, resulting in sealing problems.

9. Compare the old hose to the replacement hose.

   Is the replacement hose correct? Yes ___ No ___

10. Lightly coat the hose nipples with nonhardening sealer.

11. Place new hose clamps over the replacement hose.

12. Install the hose on the hose nipples.

13. Position and tighten the hose clamps.

14. Refill the system with the proper coolant, following the procedures in Job 36. Many modern vehicles use special long-life coolant. Do not mix coolant types.

15. Start the engine and check for leaks.

Figure 37-3. Compress the tabs on the hose clamp to loosen the clamp.

Name_____

Job Wrap-Up

☐   1. Clean the work area, including any coolant spills, and return any equipment to storage.

☐   2. Did you encounter any problems during this procedure? Yes ____ No ____

If Yes, describe the problems:

_____

_____

What did you do to correct the problems?

_____

_____

☐   3. Have your instructor check your work and sign this job sheet.

Performance Evaluation—Instructor Use Only

Did the student complete the job in the time allotted? Yes ____ No ____

If No, which steps were not completed? _____

How would you rate this student's overall performance on this job?_____

5–Excellent, 4–Good, 3–Satisfactory, 2–Unsatisfactory, 1–Poor

Comments: _____

_____

_____

INSTRUCTOR'S SIGNATURE_____

Notes

Project 10: Job 38—Replace a Coolant Pump

After completing this job, you will be able to remove and replace a coolant pump.

Instructions

As you read the job instructions, answer the questions and perform the tasks. Record your answers using complete sentences. Consult the proper service literature and ask your instructor for help as needed.

> ⚠ **Warning:** Before performing this job, review all pertinent safety information in the text and discuss safety procedures with your instructor.

Procedures

- ☐ 1. Obtain a vehicle to be used in this job. Your instructor may direct you to perform this job on a shop vehicle.
- ☐ 2. Gather the tools needed to perform the following job. Refer to the tools and materials list at the beginning of the project.

Remove and Replace the Coolant Pump

- ☐ 1. Ensure that the engine and cooling system are sufficiently cool (cooling system not under pressure) to allow the radiator cap to be safely removed.
- ☐ 2. Remove the radiator cap, then locate the radiator drain plug.
- ☐ 3. Place a suitable container under the drain plug.
- ☐ 4. Open the radiator drain plug. Ensure that coolant drains into the container.

> ⚠ **Warning:** Clean up any coolant spills. Antifreeze is poisonous to people and animals.

- ☐ 5. Allow the coolant to drain out so that the level of coolant in the engine is below the level of the coolant pump. It is not necessary to remove all of the coolant.
- ☐ 6. Loosen and detach the cooling system hoses at the coolant pump. If you did not drain all of the coolant, keep the lower radiator hose above the level of fluid in the engine.
- ☐ 7. Remove any accessories or brackets blocking the coolant pump.
- ☐ 8. Loosen and remove the pump drive belt.
- ☐ 9. Loosen and remove the pump pulley fasteners. Then, remove the pulley and, if necessary, the fan.
- ☐ 10. Remove the fasteners holding the coolant pump to the engine.
- ☐ 11. Remove the coolant pump from the engine. It may be necessary to carefully pry on the pump to loosen it.
- ☐ 12. Remove any gasket material from the engine-to-pump sealing areas. Be careful not to gouge or nick the metal surfaces.

☐ 13. Compare the old and replacement pumps. Check the following:

Do the pump sizes match? Yes ___ No ___

Do the pump bolt patterns match? Yes ___ No ___

Do the direction of pump impellers match? Yes ___ No ___

Do the pump shaft lengths match? Yes ___ No ___

If the pumps do not match, explain why:

_____

_____

> 🔧 **Caution:** If the pump has heavy rust deposits, as in **Figure 38-1**, be sure to flush the cooling system before releasing the vehicle. If you do not flush the system, rust deposits will ruin the new pump.

☐ 14. If specified, coat the sealing surfaces on the coolant pump and engine with nonhardening sealer.

☐ 15. Install the new coolant pump gasket on the engine.

☐ 16. Place the coolant pump on the engine and install the pump fasteners. If the fasteners extend into the coolant passage, the threads should be coated with nonhardening sealer.

☐ 17. Tighten the pump fasteners in an alternating pattern to evenly draw the pump to the engine. Be careful not to overtighten the fasteners.

☐ 18. Install the pump pulley and, if necessary, the fan. Loosely install the pulley fasteners.

☐ 19. Install the pump drive belt.

☐ 20. Tighten the pump pulley fasteners.

☐ 21. Reinstall any accessories or brackets that had to be removed to access the coolant pump. Make sure the belts are properly adjusted.

☐ 22. Refill the system with the proper coolant, following the procedures in Job 36. Many modern vehicles use special long-life coolant. Do not mix coolant types.

☐ 23. Start the engine and check for leaks and proper pump operation.

Figure 38-1. Rust deposits on this pump impeller indicate that the cooling system has not been maintained. The system must be flushed or the new pump will be damaged.

Name _____

Replace a Timing Gear-Driven Coolant Pump

☐ 1. Drain the engine coolant.

☐ 2. Remove any exhaust system and wiring blocking access to the timing cover.

☐ 3. Remove the timing cover fasteners and the cover.

☐ 4. Relieve tension on the timing chain tensioner.

☐ 5. Remove the lower radiator hose from the coolant pump or coolant pump housing, as necessary.

☐ 6. Remove the coolant pump housing if one is used.

☐ 7. Remove the fasteners holding the coolant pump to the engine.

☐ 8. Remove the coolant pump by maneuvering the driven gear out of engagement with the timing chain and sliding the pump out of the engine.

☐ 9. Scrape all mounting surfaces as needed. Most gear driven pumps will have at least two gasket surfaces, **Figure 38-2**.

☐ 10. Compare the old and new pumps.

Do the pumps match? Yes ___ No ___

If No, consult your instructor.

☐ 11. Place the new gaskets in position using sealer as recommended.

☐ 12. Place the coolant pump in position on the engine making sure that the driven gear is lined up with the timing chain.

☐ 13. Install and tighten the coolant pump fasteners.

☐ 14. Install the coolant pump housing gaskets, using sealer as necessary.

☐ 15. Reinstall the coolant pump housing.

☐ 16. Reinstall the lower radiator hose on the coolant pump housing.

☐ 17. Ensure that the timing chain is properly aligned with the pump, then allow the timing chain tensioner to assume its original position.

☐ 18. Using gaskets and sealer as needed, reinstall the timing chain cover.

☐ 19. Reinstall exhaust system components and wiring as necessary.

Figure 38-2. This pump has two gasket surfaces, one that seals in coolant around the pump impeller and one that seals in oil around the timing gear.

Caution: If any coolant has entered the engine oil pan, drain and replace the oil before proceeding. Antifreeze in the oil can badly damage an engine.

☐ 20. Replace the coolant and start the engine.
☐ 21. With the engine running, bleed the cooling system and check the pump for leaks.

Replace an Electrically Driven Coolant Pump

☐ 1. Disconnect the vehicle battery negative cable.
☐ 2. Drain the engine coolant.
☐ 3. Remove any engine or system components blocking access to the coolant pump.
☐ 4. Remove hoses from the coolant pump as needed.
☐ 5. Disconnect the pump motor's electrical connectors.
☐ 6. Remove the fasteners holding the coolant pump to the engine.
☐ 7. Remove the coolant pump from the engine.
☐ 8. Scrape all mounting surfaces as needed.
☐ 9. Compare the new and old pumps.

Do the pumps match? Yes ___ No ___

If No, consult your instructor before proceeding.

☐ 10. Place new gaskets in position using sealer as recommended.
☐ 11. Place the coolant pump in position on the engine.
☐ 12. Install and tighten the coolant pump fasteners.
☐ 13. Reconnect the pump motor's electrical connectors.
☐ 14. Reinstall any other components that were removed.
☐ 15. Reinstall hoses as needed.
☐ 16. Replace the coolant and reconnect the battery negative cable.
☐ 17. Start the engine and bleed the cooling system with the engine running.
☐ 18. Check the coolant pump for leaks.
☐ 19. Clean up any spilled coolant.

Project 10: Job 38 *(continued)*

Job Wrap-Up

☐   1. Clean the work area and return any equipment to storage.

☐   2. Did you encounter any problems during this procedure? Yes ____ No ____
      If Yes, describe the problems:

_____

_____

      What did you do to correct the problems?

_____

_____

☐   3. Have your instructor check your work and sign this job sheet.

Performance Evaluation—Instructor Use Only

Did the student complete the job in the time allotted? Yes ____ No ____

If No, which steps were not completed? _____

How would you rate this student's overall performance on this job?_____

5–Excellent, 4–Good, 3–Satisfactory, 2–Unsatisfactory, 1–Poor

Comments: _____

_____

_____

INSTRUCTOR'S SIGNATURE_____

Notes

Project 10: Job 39—Replace a Radiator

After completing this job, you will be able to remove and replace a radiator.

Instructions

As you read the job instructions, answer the questions and perform the tasks. Record your answers using complete sentences. Consult the proper service literature and ask your instructor for help as needed.

> ⚠ **Warning:** Before performing this job, review all pertinent safety information in the text and discuss safety procedures with your instructor.

Procedures

☐ 1. Obtain a vehicle to be used in this job. Your instructor may direct you to perform this job on a shop vehicle.

☐ 2. Gather the tools needed to perform the following job. Refer to the tools and materials list at the beginning of the project.

☐ 3. Ensure that the engine and cooling system are sufficiently cool (cooling system not under pressure) to allow the radiator cap to be safely removed.

☐ 4. Remove the radiator cap, then locate the radiator drain plug.

☐ 5. Place a suitable container under the drain plug.

☐ 6. Open the radiator drain plug. Ensure that coolant drains into the container.

> ⚠ **Warning:** Clean up any coolant spills. Antifreeze is poisonous to people and animals.

☐ 7. Allow as much coolant to drain out as possible.

☐ 8. Remove the upper and lower radiator hoses, any heater hoses attached to the radiator, and the coolant recovery system hose.

☐ 9. Remove any electrical connectors at the radiator tanks.

☐ 10. Remove the transmission and engine oil cooler lines, if present.

☐ 11. Remove any shrouds or other parts that prevent access to the radiator. In **Figure 39-1**, an upper fan shroud is being removed. **Figure 39-2** shows an arrangement in which the upper motor mounts must be removed to gain access to the radiator.

☐ 12. Where applicable, remove the fasteners holding the electric fan assembly to the radiator, and then remove the fan assembly.

☐ 13. Remove the fasteners and brackets holding the radiator to the vehicle.

Figure 39-1. Once this upper radiator shroud is removed, the radiator can be pulled up and out of the vehicle.

Figure 39-2. On this vehicle, two upper engine mounts must be removed to gain access to the radiator.

☐ 14. Lift the radiator from the vehicle. Compare the original and replacement radiators.

   Do the sizes match? Yes ___ No ___

   Do the shapes match? Yes ___ No ___

   Are the hose nipples in the same positions? Yes ___ No ___

   Are the cooler lines and electrical fittings in the same positions? Yes ___ No ___

   Is the drain plug/petcock in the same location? Yes ___ No ___

   If the radiators do not match, describe how they differ:

   _____

   _____

☐ 15. Transfer any parts, such as coolant level switches, between the original and replacement radiators.

Project 10: Job 39 *(continued)*

Note: Many new radiators require that you transfer the drain petcock or plug from the old radiator.

☐ 16. Place the radiator in position in the vehicle. Make sure that the radiator is properly positioned and seated.

☐ 17. Install the attaching brackets.

☐ 18. Install the electric fan assembly, if necessary.

☐ 19. Install the transmission and engine oil cooler lines, if used.

☐ 20. Install any sensor electrical connectors that were disconnected.

☐ 21. Install the upper and lower radiator hoses, the coolant recovery system hose, and any heater hoses.

☐ 22. Reinstall any shrouds or other parts that were removed to access the radiator.

☐ 23. Refill the system with the proper coolant following the procedures in Job 36. Many modern vehicles use special long-life coolant. Do not mix coolant types.

☐ 24. Start the engine and check for leaks. Bleed the system as necessary. See Job 36 for bleeding procedures.

Job Wrap-Up

☐ 1. Clean the work area, including any coolant spills, and return any equipment to storage.

☐ 2. Did you encounter any problems during this procedure? Yes ____ No ____

If Yes, describe the problems:

_____

_____

What did you do to correct the problems?

_____

_____

☐ 3. Have your instructor check your work and sign this job sheet.

Performance Evaluation—Instructor Use Only

Did the student complete the job in the time allotted? Yes ___ No ___

If No, which steps were not completed? _____

How would you rate this student's overall performance on this job?_____

5–Excellent, 4–Good, 3–Satisfactory, 2–Unsatisfactory, 1–Poor

Comments: _____

_____

_____

INSTRUCTOR'S SIGNATURE_____

Project 10: Job 40—Remove and Replace a Thermostat

After completing this job, you will be able to remove and replace a thermostat.

Instructions

As you read the job instructions, answer the questions and perform the tasks. Record your answers using complete sentences. Consult the proper service literature and ask your instructor for help as needed.

> **Warning:** Before performing this job, review all pertinent safety information in the text and discuss safety procedures with your instructor.

Procedures

- ☐ 1. Obtain a vehicle to be used in this job. Your instructor may direct you to perform this job on a shop vehicle.
- ☐ 2. Gather the tools needed to perform the following job. Refer to the tools and materials list at the beginning of the project.
- ☐ 3. Ensure that the engine and cooling system are sufficiently cool (cooling system not under pressure) to allow the radiator cap to be safely removed.
- ☐ 4. Remove the radiator cap, then locate the radiator drain plug.
- ☐ 5. Place a suitable container under the drain plug.
- ☐ 6. Open the radiator drain plug. Ensure that coolant drains into the container.

> **Warning:** Clean up any coolant spills. Antifreeze is poisonous to people and animals.

- ☐ 7. Allow coolant to drain out so that the level of coolant in the engine is below the level of the thermostat. It is not necessary to remove all of the coolant.
- ☐ 8. Loosen the upper radiator hose clamp and remove the hose from the thermostat housing.
- ☐ 9. Remove the fasteners holding the thermostat housing to the engine and remove the housing. The thermostat should now be visible. See **Figure 40-1**.
- ☐ 10. Remove the thermostat from the engine.
- ☐ 11. Remove any gasket material from sealing areas on the engine and thermostat housing. You may wish to stuff a rag in the thermostat housing to prevent any debris from entering the coolant passages.

> **Note:** The following step is optional and may be assigned by your instructor.

Figure 40-1. On V-type engines, the thermostat is usually located at the front of the engine between the cylinder banks. On inline engines, thermostats are usually located near the upper radiator hose at the front of the engine.

☐ 12. Test the thermostat by suspending it in a water-filled container over a burner or other source of heat. The thermostat should not touch the sides of the container. Place a thermometer in the water and observe the thermostat as the water is heated. If the thermostat does not begin to open at its rated temperature, or is not fully open before the water begins boiling, it is defective.

☐ 13. If the thermostat is being replaced, compare the old and new thermostats. The new thermostat should be the same size as the original thermostat. The thermostat opening temperature should match the manufacturer's specifications. This temperature is usually stamped on the thermostatic element, as shown in **Figure 40-2.**

Do the sizes match? Yes ___ No ___

Do the opening temperatures match? Yes ___ No ___

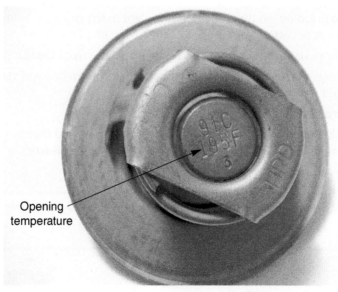

Figure 40-2. The opening temperature is usually stamped on the thermostatic element of the thermostat. Most thermostats have both Fahrenheit and Celsius values.

Project 10: Job 40 *(continued)*

> **Caution:** Do *not* install a thermostat with a lower operating temperature than the original thermostat. This will affect emissions control operations and may set a trouble code on OBD II–equipped vehicles.

☐ 14. Place the thermostat in position. The heat-sensing element should face the interior of the engine. Is the thermostat installed properly? Yes ___ No ___

☐ 15. If specified, coat the thermostat housing and engine sealing surfaces with nonhardening sealer.

☐ 16. Install the thermostat gasket on the engine.

☐ 17. Place the thermostat housing on the engine and install the housing fasteners. If the fasteners extend into the coolant passage, the threads should be coated with nonhardening sealer.

☐ 18. Tighten the thermostat housing fasteners in an alternating pattern to prevent distortion. Be careful not to overtighten the fasteners. Overtightening the fasteners can distort the housing, resulting in leaks, and may break the housing.

☐ 19. Refill the system with the proper coolant, following the procedures in Job 36. Many modern vehicles use special long-life coolant. Do not mix coolant types.

☐ 20. Start the engine and check for leaks and proper thermostat operation.

Job Wrap-Up

☐ 1. Clean the work area, including coolant spills, and return any equipment to storage.

☐ 2. Did you encounter any problems during this procedure? Yes ___ No ___
If Yes, describe the problems:

_____

_____

What did you do to correct the problems?

_____

_____

☐ 3. Have your instructor check your work and sign this job sheet.

Project 10: Job 40 (continued)

Performance Evaluation—Instructor Use Only

Did the student complete the job in the time allotted? Yes ___ No ___

If No, which steps were not completed? _____

How would you rate this student's overall performance on this job?_____

5–Excellent, 4–Good, 3–Satisfactory, 2–Unsatisfactory, 1–Poor

Comments: _____

_____

_____

INSTRUCTOR'S SIGNATURE_____